ℰꙩ **Presentation Page** ℭ℘

Presented by

———————————————————

Presented to

———————————————————

❧ 123 Glorious Hymns ❧
Every Christian Should Know

I wept at the beauty of your hymns and canticles,
and was powerfully moved at the sweet sound of your
church singing. These sounds flowed into my ears,
and the truth streamed into my heart.

Augustine of Hippo

NEARER, MY GOD, TO THEE

Nearer, my God, to Thee, nearer to Thee!
E'en though it be a cross that raiseth me,
Still all my song shall be, nearer, my God, to Thee.

> *Refrain*
> *Nearer, my God, to Thee,*
> *Nearer to Thee!*

Though like the wanderer, the sun gone down,
Darkness be over me, my rest a stone.
Yet in my dreams I'd be nearer, my God to Thee. *Refrain*

There let the way appear, steps unto Heav'n;
All that Thou sendest me, in mercy given;
Angels to beckon me nearer, my God, to Thee. *Refrain*

Or, if on joyful wing cleaving the sky,
Sun, moon, and stars forgot, upward I'll fly,
Still all my song shall be, nearer, my God, to Thee. *Refrain*

There in my Father's home, safe and at rest,
There in my Savior's love, perfectly blest;
Age after age to be, nearer my God to Thee. *Refrain*

About the writer: Sarah Flower Adams was born in Harlow, England in 1805 and died in London in 1848. She was the youngest daughter of Benjamin Flower, editor and proprietor of the *Cambridge Intelligencer*. In 1834 she married John Brydges Adams, a civil engineer and inventor. She had a gift for lyric poetry and wrote thirteen hymns for her pastor, the Reverend William Johnson Fox, an Independent minister. These were all published in *Hymns and Anthems*, London, 1841. **Key Verses:** At sundown he arrived at a good place to set up camp and stopped there for the night. Jacob found a stone for a pillow and lay down to sleep. As he slept, he dreamed of a stairway that reached from earth to heaven. And he saw the angels of God going up and down on it. –Genesis 28:11, 12

◆ 2 ◆

THE SPACIOUS FIRMAMENT ON HIGH

The spacious firmament on high,
With all the blue ethereal sky,
And spangled heavens, a shining frame
Their great Original proclaim.
Th'unwearied sun, from day to day,
Does his Creator's powers display,
And publishes to every land
The work of an Almighty Hand.

Soon as the evening shades prevail
The moon takes up the wondrous tale,
And nightly to the listening earth
Repeats the story of her birth;
While all the stars that round her burn
And all the planets in their turn,
Confirm the tidings as they roll,
And spread the truth from pole to pole.

What though in solemn silence all
Move round the dark terrestrial ball?
What though no real voice nor sound
Amid the radiant orbs be found?
In reason's ear they all rejoice,
And utter forth a glorious voice,
Forever singing as they shine,
"The hand that made us is divine."

About the writer: Joseph Addison was born in 1672, the son of Reverend
Lancelot Addison, Dean of Lichfield, England. He was educated at Oxford
and early developed poetic talent. His literary contributions were made
chiefly to various magazines. He is the author of five hymns, all of which
appeared in the *Spectator* in 1712. Addison died in 1719. At the time of his
death he was contemplating a poetic version of the Psalms. "The piety of
Addison," wrote a contemporary, "was in truth of a singularly cheerful kind.

The feeling which predominates in all his devotional writings is gratitude; and on that goodness to which he ascribed all the happiness of his life he relied in the hour of death with a love which casteth out fear." **Key Verse:** The heavens tell of the glory of God. The skies display his marvelous craftsmanship. –Psalm 19:1

◆ 3 ◆

ALL THINGS BRIGHT AND BEAUTIFUL

Refrain
All things bright and beautiful,
All creatures great and small,
All things wise and wonderful:
The Lord God made them all.

The cold wind in the winter,
The pleasant summer sun,
The ripe fruits in the garden,
He made them every one. *Refrain*

Each little flower that opens,
Each little bird that sings,
He made their glowing colors,
He made their tiny wings. *Refrain*

The tall trees in the greenwood,
The meadows where we play,
The rushes by the water,
To gather every day. *Refrain*

The purple headed mountains,
The river running by,
The sunset and the morning
That brightens up the sky. *Refrain*

He gave us eyes to see them,
And lips that we might tell
How great is God Almighty,
Who has made all things well.
Refrain

About the writer: Cecil Frances Alexander was born in Ireland in 1823. In 1850 she married Reverend William Alexander, Bishop of Derry. She was the author of several books of poetry. Among them were: *Verses for Holy Seasons*, 1846; *Hymns for Little Children*, 1848; *Hymns Descriptive and Devotional*, 1858; and *The Legend of the Golden Prayers*, 1859. She died in 1895. **Key Verse:** Then God looked over all he had made, and he saw that it was excellent in every way. This all happened on the sixth day. –Genesis 1:31

◆ 4 ◆

TEN THOUSAND TIMES TEN THOUSAND
Ten thousand times ten thousand in sparkling raiment bright,

The armies of the ransomed saints throng up the steeps of light;
'Tis finished, all is finished, their fight with death and sin;
Fling open wide the golden gates, and let the victors in.

What rush of alleluias fills all the earth and sky!
What ringing of a thousand harps bespeaks the triumph nigh!
O day, for which creation and all its tribes were made;
O joy, for all its former woes a thousandfold repaid!

Bring near Thy great salvation, Thou Lamb for sinners slain;
Fill up the roll of Thine elect, then take Thy power, and reign;
Appear, Desire of nations, Thine exiles long for home;
Show in the heaven Thy promised sign; Thou Prince and Savior, come.

About the writer: Henry Alford, widely known as the author of *The Greek Testament with Notes*, was born in London in 1810. He wrote the following dedication in his Bible at the age of 16: "I do this day, in the presence of God and my own soul, renew my covenant with God, and solemnly determine henceforth to become his and to do his work as far as in me lies." He was educated at Trinity College, Cambridge, ordained in 1833, and soon made a reputation as an eloquent preacher and sound biblical critic. He was appointed Dean of Canterbury in 1857, which distinction he held to the day of his death in 1871. **Key Verse:** Then I looked again, and I heard the singing of thousands and millions of angels around the throne and the living beings and the elders. –Revelation 5:11

◆ **5** ◆

OUR BLEST REDEEMER, ERE HE BREATHED
Our blest Redeemer, ere He breathed
His tender last farewell,
A Guide, a Comforter, bequeathed
With us to dwell.

He came in tongues of living flame
To teach, convince, subdue,

All powerful as the wind He came
As viewless too.

And every virtue we possess,
And every conquest won,
And every thought of holiness,
Are His alone.

Spirit of purity and grace,
Our weakness, pitying, see:
O make our hearts Thy dwelling place
And worthier Thee.

About the writer: Harriet Auber was born in 1773 and died in 1862. She led a quiet life, writing much but publishing only one volume. The full title of her book was *The Spirit of the Psalms: A Compressed Version of Select Portions of the Psalms of David*. It was published anonymously in 1829.
Key Verse: But it is actually best for you that I go away, because if I don't, the Counselor won't come. If I do go away, he will come because I will send him to you. –John 16:7

◆ 6 ◆

THE KING OF LOVE MY SHEPHERD IS

The King of love my Shepherd is,
Whose goodness faileth never,
I nothing lack if I am His
And He is mine forever.

Where streams of living water flow
My ransomed soul He leadeth,
And where the verdant
        pastures grow,
With food celestial feedeth.

Thou spread'st a table in my sight;
Thy unction grace bestoweth;
And O what transport of delight
From Thy pure chalice floweth!

And so through all the length of days
Thy goodness faileth never;
Good Shepherd, may I sing Thy
        praise
Within Thy house forever.

About the writer: Sir Henry Williams Baker, an eminent English clergyman, was born in London in 1821. Educated at Trinity College, Cambridge, he took holy orders in 1844 and became vicar of Monkland, Herefordshire in 1851. He was editor in chief of *Hymns Ancient and Modern*, to which he contributed several of his hymns. A contemporary wrote, "Of his hymns four only are in the highest strain of jubilation, another four are bright and cheerful, and the remainder are very tender but exceedingly plaintive, sometimes even to sadness." He died in 1877. His last audible words were a quotation of the third stanza of his rendering of the twenty-third Psalm: "Perverse and foolish, oft I strayed; But yet in love He sought me, And on His shoulder gently laid; And home rejoicing brought me." **Key Verse:** The LORD is my shepherd; I have everything I need. –Psalm 23:1

◆ 7 ◆

HAIL, THOU ONCE DESPISED JESUS
Hail, Thou once despisèd Jesus! Hail, Thou Galilean King!
Thou didst suffer to release us; Thou didst free salvation bring.
Hail, Thou universal Savior, Who hast borne our sin and shame!
By Thy merits we find favor; life is given through Thy Name.

Paschal Lamb, by God appointed, all our sins on Thee were laid;
By almighty love anointed, Thou hast full atonement made.
Every sin may be forgiven through the virtue of Thy blood;
Opened is the gate of heaven, reconciled are we with God.

Jesus, hail! enthroned in glory, there forever to abide;
All the heavenly hosts adore Thee, seated at Thy Father's side.
There for sinners Thou art pleading; there Thou dost our place prepare;
Thou for saints art interceding till in glory they appear.

Worship, honor, power and blessing Christ is worthy to receive;
Loudest praises, without ceasing, right it is for us to give.
Help, ye bright angelic spirits, bring your sweetest, noblest lays;
Help to sing of Jesus' merits, help to chant Emmanuel's praise!

About the writer: John Bakewell, a Wesleyan lay preacher, was born in Derbyshire, England in 1721. He was made a lay preacher in 1749 and proved to be one of John Wesley's most efficient workers. He was for

several years Master of the Greenwich Royal Park Academy. He died in
1819 and was buried in City Road Chapel not far from the tomb of Wesley.
The epitaph upon his tombstone states that "he adorned the doctrines of
God our Saviour eighty years, and preached his glorious gospel about seventy
years." **Key Verse:** He was despised and rejected–a man of sorrows,
acquainted with bitterest grief. We turned our backs on him and looked the
other way when he went by. He was despised, and we did not care. –Isaiah
53:3

♦ 8 ♦

ONWARD, CHRISTIAN SOLDIERS
Onward, Christian soldiers, marching as to war,
With the cross of Jesus going on before.
Christ, the royal Master, leads against the foe;
Forward into battle see His banners go!
>   *Refrain*
>   *Onward, Christian soldiers, marching as to war,*
>   *With the cross of Jesus going on before.*

At the sign of triumph Satan's host doth flee;
On then, Christian soldiers, on to victory!
Hell's foundations quiver at the shout of praise;
Brothers lift your voices, loud your anthems raise. *Refrain*

Like a mighty army moves the church of God;
Brothers, we are treading where the saints have trod;
We are not divided, all one body we,
One in hope and doctrine, one in charity. *Refrain*

Crowns and thrones may perish, kingdoms rise and wane,
But the church of Jesus constant will remain.
Gates of hell can never gainst that church prevail;
We have Christ's own promise, and that cannot fail. *Refrain*

Onward then, ye people, join our happy throng,
Blend with ours your voices in the triumph song.

Glory, laud and honor unto Christ the King,
This through countless ages men and angels sing. *Refrain*

About the writer: Sabine Baring-Gould, an English clergyman, was born in Exeter, England in 1834. He was educated at Clare College, Cambridge. His prose works included *Lives of the Saints* in fifteen volumes, 1872-1877. He was the author of a number of fine hymns, the best-known of which is "Onward, Christian soldiers." **Key Verse:** He said, "Listen, King Jehoshaphat! Listen, all you people of Judah and Jerusalem! This is what the LORD says: Do not be afraid! Don't be discouraged by this mighty army, for the battle is not yours, but God's. –2 Chronicles 20:15

♦ 9 ♦

WALK IN THE LIGHT
Walk in the light: so shalt thou know
That fellowship of love
His Spirit only can bestow
Who reigns in light above.

Walk in the light: and sin abhorred
Shall ne'er defile again;
The blood of Jesus Christ thy Lord
Shall cleanse from every stain.

Walk in the light: and e'en the tomb
No fearful shade shall wear;
Glory shall chase away its gloom,
For Christ has conquered there.

Walk in the light: and thine shall be
A path, though thorny, bright;
For God, by grace, shall dwell in thee,
And God Himself is light.

About the writer: Bernard Barton was born in London in 1784 and was educated at a Quaker school in Ipswich. In 1810 he was employed at a local bank in Suffolk, where he remained forty years. He was the author of 10 small volumes of verse between 1812 and 1845. From these books some twenty pieces have come into common use as hymns. He died in Woodbridge in 1849. His daughter published his *Poems and Letters*, 1849, after his death.

Key Verse: This is the message he has given us to announce to you: God is light and there is no darkness in him at all. –1 John 1:5

♦ 10 ♦

O, FOR A FAITH THAT WILL NOT SHRINK

O, for a faith that will not shrink,
Though pressed by every foe,
That will not tremble on the brink
Of any earthly woe!

That will not murmur nor complain
Beneath the chastening rod,
But, in the hour of grief or pain,
Will lean upon its God.

A faith that shines more bright and clear
When tempests rage without;
That when in danger knows no fear,
In darkness feels no doubt.

A faith that keeps the narrow way
Till life's last hour is fled,
And with a pure and heavenly ray
Lights up a dying bed.

Lord, give me such a faith as this,
And then, whate'er may come,
I'll taste, e'en here, the hallowed bliss
Of an eternal home.

About the writer: William Hiley Bathurst, a clergyman for the Church of England, was born in Bristol, England in 1796. He was the son of Charles Bragge, who was member of Parliament for Bristol, and who, upon inheriting his uncle's estate, assumed his name, Bathurst. He graduated from Christ Church College, Oxford, and was ordained a priest in 1819. The following year he became rector of Barwick-in-Elmet, Yorkshire, where he remained for 32 years. His biographer, speaking of these years of ministerial service, wrote: "Faithfully devoting himself to the spiritual welfare of his parishioners, he greatly endeared himself to them all by his eminent piety, his great simplicity of character, his tender love, and his abundant generosity." In 1863, upon the death of his older brother, he moved to the family estate in Gloucestershire where he died in 1877. **Key Verse:** One day the apostles said to the Lord, "We need more faith; tell us how to get it." –Luke 17:5

♦ 11 ♦

LORD, IT BELONGS NOT TO MY CARE

Lord, it belongs not to my care
Whether I die or live;
To love and serve Thee is my share,
And this Thy grace must give.

If life be long, I will be glad,
That I may long obey;
If short, yet why should I be sad
To welcome endless day?

Christ leads me through
    no darker rooms
Than He went through before;
He that unto God's kingdom comes
Must enter by this door.

Then I shall end my sad complaints
And weary sinful days,
And join with the triumphant saints
That sing my Savior's praise.

My knowledge of that life is small,
The eye of faith is dim;
But 'tis enough that Christ
    knows all,
And I shall be with Him.

About the writer: Richard Baxter, a Puritan minister and voluminous author of the seventeenth century, wrote the devotional masterpiece *Call to the Unconverted and his Saint's Everlasting Rest*. At 25 he entered the ministry and was appointed to the parish of Kidderminster (1640). Here he remained until "for conscience' sake" he, along with many other Nonconformist clergy, was driven out by the "Act of Uniformity" passed in 1662. He ceased to preach but was caught holding family prayers "with more than four persons." He was arrested and imprisoned for six months. When released he lived in retirement until 1672 when the "Act of Indulgence" gave him liberty to preach and to publish again. **Key Verse:** Trust in the LORD always, for the LORD GOD is the eternal Rock. –Isaiah 26:4

◆ 12 ◆

COME, HOLY SPIRIT, COME

Come, Holy Spirit, come,
With energy divine,
And on this poor, benighted soul
With beams of mercy shine.

O melt this frozen heart;
This stubborn will subdue;
Each evil passion overcome,
And form me all anew!

The profit will be mine,
But Thine shall be the praise;
And unto Thee will I devote
The remnant of my days.

About the writer: Benjamin Beddome, an English Baptist minister, was born in Warwickshire, England in 1717. He was apprenticed to an apothecary in Bristol but when he was 20 he began to prepare for the ministry. In 1743 he was ordained and became the pastor of a small Baptist Church at Bourton. Here he remained until his death in 1795. It was a frequent custom with him to write a hymn to be sung after his morning sermon. A volume of his hymns, over eight hundred in number, was published in 1818. **Key Verse:** But I will send you the Counselor–the Spirit of truth. He will come to you from the Father and will tell you all about me. –John 15:26

◆ 13 ◆

O SACRED HEAD, NOW WOUNDED

O sacred Head, now wounded, with grief and shame weighed down,
Now scornfully surrounded with thorns, Thine only crown;
How pale Thou art with anguish, with sore abuse and scorn!
How does that visage languish, which once was bright as morn!

What Thou, my Lord, hast suffered, was all for sinners' gain;
Mine, mine was the transgression, but Thine the deadly pain.
Lo, here I fall, my Savior! 'Tis I deserve Thy place;
Look on me with Thy favor, vouchsafe to me Thy grace.

Men mock and taunt and jeer Thee, Thou noble countenance,
Though mighty worlds shall fear Thee and flee before Thy glance.
How art thou pale with anguish, with sore abuse and scorn!
How doth Thy visage languish that once was bright as morn!

My Shepherd, now receive me; my Guardian, own me Thine.
Great blessings Thou didst give me, O source of gifts divine.
Thy lips have often fed me with words of truth and love;
Thy Spirit oft hath led me to heavenly joys above.

Here I will stand beside Thee, from Thee I will not part;
O Savior, do not chide me! When breaks Thy loving heart,
When soul and body languish in death's cold, cruel grasp,
Then, in Thy deepest anguish, Thee in mine arms I'll clasp.

The joy can never be spoken, above all joys beside,
When in Thy body broken I thus with safety hide.
O Lord of Life, desiring Thy glory now to see,
Beside Thy cross expiring, I'd breathe my soul to Thee.

Be Thou my consolation, my shield when I must die;
Remind me of Thy passion when my last hour draws nigh.
Mine eyes shall then behold Thee, upon Thy cross shall dwell,
My heart by faith enfolds Thee. Who dieth thus dies well.

About the writer: Bernard of Clairvaux, an eminent monk, theologian, scholar, preacher, and poet, was born in Burgundy, France in 1091. Aletta, his mother, was a pious woman and consecrated her son to God from his birth. Being naturally fond of seclusion, meditation, and study he sought a home in the cloister. At 22 he entered the small monastery of Citeaux and later founded and made famous that of Clairvaux. Kings and popes sought his advice since his enthusiasm and impassioned eloquence were all but irresistible. He died in 1153. Luther greatly admired him and thought him "the greatest monk that ever lived." His published works are in five folio volumes. **Key Verse:** They made a crown of long, sharp thorns and put it on his head, and they placed a stick in his right hand as a scepter. Then they knelt before him in mockery, yelling, "Hail! King of the Jews!" –Matthew 27:29

◆ 14 ◆

WHEN TIME SEEMS SHORT AND DEATH IS NEAR

When time seems short, and death is near,
And I am pressed by doubt and fear,
And sins, an overflowing tide,
Assail my peace on every side,
This thought my refuge still shall be,
I know my Savior died for me.

His name is Jesus, and He died—
For guilty sinners crucified;
Content to die, that He might win
Their ransom from the death of sin.
No sinner worse than I can be,
Therefore I know He died for me.

I read God's holy Word, and find
Great truths which far transcend my mind
And little do I know beside
Of thought so high and deep and wide.
This is my best theology—
I know the Savior died for me.

My faith is weak, but 'tis Thy gift;
Thou canst my helpless soul uplift,
And say, "Thy bonds of death are riv'n,
Thy sins by Me are all forgiv'n,
And thou shalt live, from guilt set free;
For I, thy Savior, died for thee."

About the writer: George Washington Bethume, a minister in the Reformed Dutch Church, was born in New York in 1805. He graduated from Dickinson College in 1823, and studied theology at Princeton. In 1827 he became pastor of a Reformed Dutch Church at Rhinebeck, New York. In 1861 he went abroad for his health. He died in Florence, Italy in 1862 suddenly after preaching. Dr. Bethune wrote occasional hymns and poems for more than 30 years. A collection of his poems, *Lays of Love and Faith*, was published in Philadelphia in 1847. **Key Verse:** But God showed his great love for us by sending Christ to die for us while we were still sinners. –Romans 5:8

◆ 15 ◆

O GOD, THE ROCK OF AGES

O God, the Rock of Ages,
Who evermore hast been,
What time the tempest rages,
Our dwelling place serene:
Before Thy first creations,
O Lord, the same as now,
To endless generations,
The everlasting Thou.

Our years are like the shadows
On sunny hills that lie,
Or grasses in the meadows
That blossom but to die;
Asleep, a dream, a story
By strangers quickly told
And unremaining glory
Of things that soon are old.

O Thou, Who dost not slumber,
Whose light grows never pale,
Teach us aright to number
Our years before they fail;
On us Thy mercy lighten,
On us Thy goodness rest,
And let Thy Spirit brighten
The hearts Thyself hast blessed.

Lord, crown our faith's endeavor
With beauty and with grace,
Till, clothed in light forever,
We see Thee face to face:
A joy no language measures,
A fountain brimming o'er,
An endless flow of pleasures,
An ocean without shore.

About the writer: Edward Henry Bickersteth, a bishop of the Church of England, was born in Islington, England in 1825. He graduated from Cambridge University and took holy orders in the Church of England in 1848. He became Dean of Gloucester in 1885, and that same year he was appointed Bishop of Exeter. He published his *Hymn Companion* in 1870. The editor of the *Dictionary of Hymnology* wrote of the collection: "Of its kind and from its theological standpoint, it is in poetic grace, literary excellence, and lyric beauty, the finest collection in the Anglican Church." He retired from active work in 1900 and died in 1906. **Key Verse:** Trust in the LORD always, for the LORD GOD is the eternal Rock. –Isaiah 26:4

◆ 16 ◆

I HEARD THE VOICE OF JESUS SAY

I heard the voice of Jesus say, "Come unto Me and rest;
Lay down, thou weary one, lay down Thy head upon My breast."
I came to Jesus as I was, weary and worn and sad;
I found in Him a resting place, and He has made me glad.

I heard the voice of Jesus say, "Behold, I freely give
The living water; thirsty one, stoop down, and drink, and live."
I came to Jesus, and I drank of that life giving stream;
My thirst was quenched, my soul revived, and now I live in Him.

I heard the voice of Jesus say, "I am this dark world's Light;
Look unto Me, thy morn shall rise, and all thy day be bright."
I looked to Jesus, and I found in Him my Star, my Sun;
And in that light of life I'll walk, till traveling days are done.

About the writer: Horatius Bonar, a distinguished Presbyterian minister, was born in Edinburgh, Scotland in 1808. He was educated at the University of Edinburgh, was ordained in 1837, and became a minister of the Established Church at Kelso. He later became one of the founders of the Free Church of Scotland. He was a voluminous writer of sacred poetry until his death in 1889. **Key Verses:** Then Jesus said, "Come to me, all of you who are weary and carry heavy burdens, and I will give you rest. Take my yoke upon you. Let me teach you, because I am humble and gentle, and you will find rest for your souls. For my yoke fits perfectly, and the burden I give you is light." – Matthew 11:28-30

◆ 17 ◆

CROWN HIM WITH MANY CROWNS

Crown Him with many crowns, the Lamb upon His throne.

Hark! How the heavenly anthem drowns all music but its own.
Awake, my soul, and sing of Him who died for thee,
And hail Him as thy matchless King through all eternity.

Crown Him the virgin's Son, the God incarnate born,
Whose arm those crimson trophies won which now His brow adorn;
Fruit of the mystic rose, as of that rose the stem;
The root whence mercy ever flows, the Babe of Bethlehem.

Crown Him the Son of God, before the worlds began,
And ye who tread where He hath trod, crown Him the Son of Man;
Who every grief hath known that wrings the human breast,
And takes and bears them for His own, that all in Him may rest.

Crown Him the Lord of life, who triumphed over the grave,
And rose victorious in the strife for those He came to save.
His glories now we sing, Who died, and rose on high,
Who died eternal life to bring, and lives that death may die.

Crown Him the Lord of peace, Whose power a scepter sways
From pole to pole, that wars may cease, and all be prayer and praise.
His reign shall know no end, and round His piercèd feet
Fair flowers of paradise extend their fragrance ever sweet.

Crown Him the Lord of love, behold His hands and side,
Those wounds, yet visible above, in beauty glorified.
No angel in the sky can fully bear that sight,
But downward bends his burning eye at mysteries so bright.

Crown Him the Lord of Heaven, enthroned in worlds above,
Crown Him the King to Whom is given the wondrous name of Love.
Crown Him with many crowns, as thrones before Him fall;
Crown Him, ye kings, with many crowns, for He is King of all.

Crown Him the Lord of lords, who over all doth reign,
Who once on earth, the incarnate Word, for ransomed sinners slain,

Now lives in realms of light, where saints with angels sing
Their songs before Him day and night, their God, Redeemer, King.

Crown Him the Lord of years, the Potentate of time,
Creator of the rolling spheres, ineffably sublime.
All hail, Redeemer, hail! For Thou has died for me;
Thy praise and glory shall not fail throughout eternity.

About the writer: Matthew Bridges was an Englishman born in Essex, England in 1800. He was educated in the Church of England but became a convert to the Catholic Church in connection with the famous Tractarian movement led by Cardinal Newman and others. For several years before his death he resided in the province of Quebec, Canada where he died in 1894. He was the author of several books including *Hymns of the Heart*, 1848. **Key Verse:** His eyes were bright like flames of fire, and on his head were many crowns. A name was written on him, and only he knew what it meant. – Revelation 19:12

◆ **18** ◆

O LITTLE TOWN OF BETHLEHEM
O little town of Bethlehem, how still we see thee lie!
Above thy deep and dreamless sleep the silent stars go by.
Yet in thy dark streets shineth the everlasting Light;
The hopes and fears of all the years are met in thee tonight.

For Christ is born of Mary, and gathered all above,
While mortals sleep, the angels keep their watch of wondering love.
O morning stars together, proclaim the holy birth,
And praises sing to God the King, and peace to men on earth!

How silently, how silently, the wondrous Gift is giv'n;
So God imparts to human hearts the blessings of His Heav'n.
No ear may hear His coming, but in this world of sin,
Where meek souls will receive Him still, the dear Christ enters in.

Where children pure and happy pray to the Blessed Child,
Where misery cries out to Thee, Son of the mother mild;
Where charity stands watching and faith holds wide the door,
The dark night wakes, the glory breaks, and Christmas comes once more.

O holy Child of Bethlehem, descend to us, we pray;
Cast out our sin, and enter in, be born in us today.
We hear the Christmas angels the great glad tidings tell;
O come to us, abide with us, our Lord Emmanuel!

About the writer: Phillips Brooks, a bishop of the Protestant Episcopal Church, was born in Boston in 1835. He graduated from Harvard College in 1855 and then attended the Episcopal School of Theology in Alexandria, Virginia. He was ordained in 1859 and became the rector of the Church of the Advent in Philadelphia. Later, in 1891, he was elected Bishop of Massachusetts but died just two years later. He wrote at least four Christmas and two Easter carols. **Key Verse:** But you, O Bethlehem Ephrathah, are only a small village in Judah. Yet a ruler of Israel will come from you, one whose origins are from the distant past. –Micah 5:2

♦ 19 ♦

I LOVE TO STEAL AWHILE AWAY
I love to steal awhile away
From every cumbering care,
And spend the hours of closing day
In humble, grateful, prayer.

I love to think on mercies past,
And future good implore,
And all my cares and sorrows cast
On God, Whom I adore.

I love by faith to take a view
Of brighter scenes in heaven;
The prospect doth my strength renew,
While here by tempests driven.

Thus, when life's toilsome day is o'er,
May its departing ray,
Be calm at this impressive hour,
And lead to endless day.

About the writer: Phoebe Hinsdale Brown was born in 1783 in Canaan, New York. Being left an orphan when only two years of age, her early life was one of want, hardship, and drudgery. At the age of nine she went to live with a relative who kept a county jail. "These were years of intense and cruel suffering," wrote her son. "The tale of her early life is a narrative of such deprivations, toil, and cruel treatment as it breaks my heart to read." Not until she was eighteen years of age did she escape from this bondage and find a home among kind and sympathetic people. Her education was limited to three months in the public school where she learned to write. She made at this time a profession of faith in Christ and joined the Congregational Church. She died in 1861. "Despite all her disadvantages," wrote her biographer, "Mrs. Brown's talents and work are superior to those of any other early female hymnist of America." **Key Verse:** Afterward he went up into the hills by himself to pray. Night fell while he was there alone. –Matthew 14:23

◆ 20 ◆

OF ALL THE THOUGHTS OF GOD
Of all the thoughts of God that are
Borne inward into souls afar,
Along the psalmist's music deep,
Now tell me if there any is,
For gift or grace surpassing this:
"He giveth His beloved sleep"?

What would we give to our beloved?
The hero's heart to be unmoved,
The poet's star tuned harp, to sweep,
The patriot's voice, to teach and rouse,
The monarch's crown, to light the brows?
He giveth His beloved sleep.

His dews drop mutely on the hill,
His cloud above it saileth still,
Though on its slope men sow and reap;
More softly than the dew is shed,
Or cloud is floated overhead,
He giveth His beloved sleep.

About the writer: Elizabeth Barrett Browning, scarcely less famous as a poet than her illustrious husband, Robert Browning, was born in London in 1809. In 1846 she and her husband moved to Italy where she lived until her death in 1861. In all literature there is no parallel case where husband and wife have each attained such distinction as poets. Beginning at eight years of age to write, she produced during the forty years of her literary life countless poems of artistic beauty that reflected her Christian faith. **Key Verse:** Afterward he went up into the hills by himself to pray. Night fell while he was there alone. –Psalm 127:2

◆ 21 ◆
DEEM NOT THAT THEY ARE BLEST ALONE
Deem not that they are blest alone
Whose days a peaceful tenor keep;
Th'anointed Son of God makes known
A blessing for the eyes that weep.

The light of smiles shall fill again
The lids that overflow with tears;
And weary hours of woe and pain
Are promises of happier years.

There is a day of sunny rest
For every dark and troubled night;
And grief shall bide an evening guest,
But joy shall come with early light.

For God has marked each sorrowing day,
And numbered every secret tear;

And heaven's long age of bliss shall pay
For all His children suffer here.

About the writer: William Cullen Bryant, American editor and poet, was born in Massachusetts in 1794. He studied law and practiced for about ten years. In 1826 he joined the staff of the *New York Evening Post* and continued to be one of its editors and proprietors until the day of his death in 1878. Many editions of his poems were published. **Key Verse:** For the Lamb who stands in front of the throne will be their Shepherd. He will lead them to the springs of life-giving water. And God will wipe away all their tears. – Revelation 7:17

◆ 22 ◆

O KING OF KINGS, O LORD OF HOSTS
O King of kings, O Lord of hosts, Whose throne is lifted high
Above the nations of the earth, the armies of the sky,
The spirits of perfected saints may give their nobler songs
And we, Thy children, worship Thee, to Whom all praise belongs.

Thou Who hast sown the sky with stars, and set Thy thoughts in gold,
Hast crowned our nation's life, and ours, with blessings manifold;
Thy mercies have been numberless; Thy love, Thy grace, Thy care,
Were wider than our utmost need, and higher than our prayer.

O King of kings, O Lord of hosts, our fathers' God and ours!
Be with us in the future years; and if the tempest lowers,
Look through the cloud with light of love, and smile our tears away
And lead us through the brightening years to heaven's eternal day.

About the writer: Henry Burton, a Methodist minister, was born in 1840 in the house where his grandmother, in 1818 organized the first Wesleyan juvenile missionary society. His parents moved to America in his boyhood and he was educated at Beloit College. After his graduation he became a local preacher in the Methodist Episcopal Church. He later moved back to London where he preached and wrote scholarly works and poetry until his death.

Key Verse: On his robe and thigh was written this title: King of kings and Lord of lords. –Revelation 19:16

◆ **23** ◆

THE HOLY ANTHEM
Alleluia! Alleluia!
Let the holy anthem rise,
And the choirs of heaven chant it
In the temple of the skies;
Let the mountains skip with gladness
And the joyful valleys ring,
With Hosannas in the highest
To our Savior and our King.

Alleluia! Alleluia!
Like the sun from out the wave,
He has risen up in triumph
From the darkness of the grave,
He's the splendor of the nations,
He's the lamp of endless day;
He's the very Lord of glory
Who is risen up today.

Alleluia! Alleluia!
Blessed Jesus make us rise,
From the life of this corruption
To the life that never dies.
May Your glory be our portion,
When the days of time are past,
And the dead shall be awakened
By the trumpet's mighty blast.

About the writer: Edward Caswell was the translator of many popular hymns. He was born in Hampshire, England in 1814 and graduated from Oxford in 1836. He became a deacon in the Church of England but resigned his ecclesiastical position in 1846 to join the Roman Catholic Church. He became a priest in the Congregation of the Oratory where he remained until his death in 1878. His biographer says: "His life was marked by earnest devotion to his clerical duties and a loving interest in the poor and the sick." **Key Verse:** He isn't here! He has been raised from the dead, just as he said would happen. Come, see where his body was lying. –Matthew 28:6

◆ 24 ◆

CHILDREN OF THE HEAVENLY KING

Children of the heavenly King,
As ye journey, sweetly sing;
Sing your Savior's worthy praise,
Glorious in His works and ways

Fear not, brethren; joyful stand
On the borders of your land;
Jesus Christ, your Father's Son,
Bids you undismayed go on.

We are traveling home to God,
In the way the fathers trod;
They are happy now, and we
Soon their happiness shall see.

Lord, obedient we would go,
Gladly leaving all below;
Only Thou our Leader be;
And we will still follow Thee.

About the writer: John Cennick was born in Berkshire, England in 1718. At the age of 17 he joined the Methodist church and became a preacher. A few years later he joined the Moravians and spent most of the remainder of his life in the northern part of Ireland. He returned to London in 1755 where he died that same year at the age of 37. His hymns were written for the Methodists and were altered and probably improved by the Wesleys. **Key Verse:** And since we are his children, we will share his treasures–for everything God gives to his Son, Christ, is ours, too. But if we are to share his glory, we must also share his suffering. –Romans 8:17

◆ 25 ◆

NEVER FURTHER THAN THY CROSS

Never further than Thy cross,
Never higher than Thy feet;
Here earth's precious things seem dross,
Here earth's bitter things grow sweet.

Gazing thus our sin we see,
Learn Thy love while gazing thus,
Sin, which laid the cross on Thee,
Love, which bore the cross for us.

Pressing onward as we can,
Still to this our hearts must tend;
Where our earliest hopes began,
There our last aspirings end.

Till amid the hosts of light,
We in Thee redeemed, complete,
Through Thy cross made pure and white,
Cast our crowns before Thy feet.

About the writer: Elizabeth Rundle Charles, the daughter of John Rundle, a banker and member of Parliament, was born in Devonshire, England in 1828. In 1851 she was married to Andrew Paton Charles, a barrister at law. She is described in *Allibone's Dictionary of Authors* as "one who had high reputation as a linguist, painter, musician, and poet." Her *Poems* were published in New York in 1867. Before her death in 1896 several of her hymns became standards for different churches. **Key Verses:** Whenever the living beings give glory and honor and thanks to the one sitting on the throne, the one who lives forever and ever, the twenty-four elders fall down and worship the one who lives forever and ever. –Revelation 4:9, 10a

◆ 26 ◆

WORK, FOR THE NIGHT IS COMING
Work, for the night is coming,
Work through the morning hours;
Work while the dew is sparkling,
Work 'mid springing flowers;
Work when the day grows brighter,
Work in the glowing sun;
Work, for the night is coming,
When man's work is done.

Work, for the night is coming,
Work through the sunny noon;
Fill brightest hours with labor,
Rest comes sure and soon.
Give every flying minute,
Something to keep in store;
Work, for the night is coming,
When man works no more.

Work, for the night is coming,
Under the sunset skies;
While their bright tints are glowing,
Work, for daylight flies.
Work till the last beam fadeth,
Fadeth to shine no more;
Work, while the night is darkening,
When man's work is o'er.

About the writer: Annie Louisa Coghill was born in Kiddermore, England in 1836. "Work, for the night is coming" was written in 1854 when she was only 18. The hymn was first printed in a Canadian newspaper. Her poems were gathered together and published in 1859 in a volume titled *Leaves from the Backwoods*. **Key Verse:** All of us must quickly carry out the tasks assigned us by the one who sent me, because there is little time left before the night falls and all work comes to an end. –John 9:4

◆ 27 ◆

RETURN, O WANDERER, RETURN
Return, O wanderer, return,
And seek an injured Father's face;
Those warm desires that in thee burn
Were kindled by reclaiming grace.

Return, O wanderer, return,
And seek a Father's melting heart,

Whose pitying eyes thy grief discern,
Whose hand can heal thine inward smart.

Return, O wanderer, return,
Thy Savior bids thy spirit live;
Go to His bleeding feet, and learn
How freely Jesus can forgive.

Return, O wanderer, return,
And wipe away the falling tear;
'Tis God who says, "No longer mourn,"
'Tis mercy's voice invites thee near.

About the writer: William Bengo Collyer was the pastor of a Congregational church from 1801, when he was ordained, until his death in 1854. He was born near London in 1782 and was educated at Homerton College, which he entered at the age of sixteen. He edited a hymn book which was published in 1812 called *Hymns Partly Collected and Partly Original*. To this book he contributed 57 of his own hymns. **Key Verse:** A person who strays from home is like a bird that strays from its nest. –Proverbs 27:8

◆ 28 ◆

HOW SHALL I FOLLOW HIM I SERVE?
How shall I follow Him I serve?
How shall I copy Him I love?
Not from the Blessed footsteps swerve,
Which lead me to His seat above?

Privations, sorrows, bitter scorn,
The life of toil, the mean abode,
The faithless kiss, the crown of thorn,
Are these the consecrated road?

O let me think how Thou didst leave
Untasted every pure delight,

To fast, to faint, to watch, to grieve,
The toilsome day, the homeless night.

To faint, to grieve, to die for me!
Thou camest, not Thyself to please;
And, dear as earthly comforts be,
Shall I not love Thee more than these?

Yes, I would count them all but loss,
To gain the notice of Thine eye:
Flesh shrinks and trembles at the cross,
But Thou canst give the victory.

About the writer: Josiah Conder was born in London in 1789. At an early age he lost the sight of his right eye. In 1832 he started a newspaper, which he continued to edit and publish until his death in 1855. He published more than a dozen scholarly volumes during his life as well as a Congregational hymn book, published in 1836. **Key Verse:** Then he said to the crowd, "If any of you wants to be my follower, you must put aside your selfish ambition, shoulder your cross daily, and follow me. –Luke 9:23

◆ 29 ◆

LET SONGS OF PRAISES FILL THE SKY
Let songs of praises fill the sky:
Christ, our ascended Lord,
Sends down His Spirit from on high
According to His Word.
All hail the day of Pentecost,
The coming of the Holy Ghost!

The Spirit by His heav'nly breath
Creates new life within;
He quickens sinners from the death
Of trespasses and sin.
All hail the day of Pentecost,
The coming of the Holy Ghost!

Come, Holy Spirit, from above
With Thy celestial fire;
Come and with flames of zeal and love
Our hearts and tongues inspire.
Be this our day of Pentecost,
The coming of the Holy Ghost!

About the writer: Thomas Cotterill, a clergyman in the Church of England, was born in Staffordshire, England in 1779. In 1817 he became perpetual curate of St. Paul's at Sheffield, where he spent the rest of his life. It was here that he met and formed a friendship with James Montgomery, the poet and hymn writer, who helped him in the preparation of a volume of hymns called *A Selection of Psalms and Hymns for Public and Private Use*. So popular was this book that it reached its eighth edition by 1819. It contained 150 psalms and 367 hymns, of which Montgomery furnished 50 and Cotterill 32. Cotterill died in 1823. **Key Verse:** When we were utterly helpless, Christ came at just the right time and died for us sinners. –Romans 5:6

◆ **30** ◆

THERE IS A FOUNTAIN FILLED WITH BLOOD

There is a fountain filled with blood drawn from Emmanuel's veins;
And sinners plunged beneath that flood lose all their guilty stains.
Lose all their guilty stains, lose all their guilty stains;
And sinners plunged beneath that flood lose all their guilty stains.

The dying thief rejoiced to see that fountain in his day;
And there have I, though vile as he, washed all my sins away.
Washed all my sins away, washed all my sins away;
And there have I, though vile as he, washed all my sins away.

Dear dying Lamb, Thy precious blood shall never lose its power
Till all the ransomed church of God be saved, to sin no more.
Be saved, to sin no more, be saved, to sin no more;
Till all the ransomed church of God be saved, to sin no more.

Then in a nobler, sweeter song, I'll sing Thy power to save,
When this poor lisping, stammering tongue lies silent in the grave.
Lies silent in the grave, lies silent in the grave;
When this poor lisping, stammering tongue lies silent in the grave.

Lord, I believe Thou hast prepared, unworthy though I be,
For me a blood bought free reward, a golden harp for me!
'Tis strung and tuned for endless years, and formed by power divine,
To sound in God the Father's ears no other name but Thine.

About the writer: William Cowper was born in Hertfordshire, England in 1731. His father, Reverend John Cowper, was a chaplain to George II. He spent ten years in Westminster School and then began reading law; abandoning it for literature after a very brief practice. He became the most distinguished poet of the English language in the latter half of the eighteenth century. Despite this he suffered from debilitating depression. In 1767 he moved to Olney, the home of John Newton. Cowper was a constant and prayerful attendant at Newton's church services; especially his cottage prayer meetings, for which nearly all of his hymns were written at Newton's request. The Olney Hymns, 1779, was their joint production; 78 of them coming from Cowper. He died in 1800. **Key Verse:** On that day a fountain will be opened for the dynasty of David and for the people of Jerusalem, a fountain to cleanse them from all their sins and defilement. –Zechariah 13:1

◆ 31 ◆

HOW BEAUTEOUS WERE THE MARKS DIVINE
How beauteous were the marks divine,
That in Thy meekness used to shine;
That lit Thy lonely pathway, trod
In wondrous love, O Son of God!

Oh, who like Thee, so calm, so bright,
So pure, so made to live in light?
Oh, who like Thee did ever go
So patient through a world of woe?

Oh, who like Thee so humbly bore
The scorn, the scoffs of men, before?
So meek, forgiving, godlike, high,
So glorious in humility?

Oh, in Thy light be mine to go,
Illumining all my way of woe!
And give me ever on the road
To trace Thy footsteps, Son of God!

About the writer: Arthur Cleveland Coxe, a bishop of the Episcopal Church, graduated from the University of New York in 1838, took orders in the ministry in 1841, and served as rector in Hartford, Baltimore, and New York City. In 1865 he was elected bishop of Western New York. He died in 1896. Bishop Coxe was the author of several small volumes of poetry and his hymns are found in many collections. **Key Verse:** But he was wounded and crushed for our sins. He was beaten that we might have peace. He was whipped, and we were healed! –Isaiah 53:5

♦ 32 ♦

A LITTLE WHILE
Oh, for the peace that floweth as a river,
Making life's desert places bloom and smile;
Oh, for the faith to grasp "Heav'n's bright forever,"
Amid the shadows of earth's "little while."

"A little while" for patient vigil keeping,
To face the storm and wrestle with the strong;
"A little while" to sow the seed with weeping,
Then bind the sheaves and sing the harvest song.

"A little while" the earthen pitcher taking,
To wayside brooks, from far off fountains fed;
Then the parched lip its thirst forever slaking
Beside the fullness of the Fountainhead.

"A little while" to keep the oil from failing,
"A little while" faith's flick'ring lamp to trim;
And then the Bridegroom's coming footsteps hailing,
We'll haste to meet Him with the bridal hymn.

About the writer: Jane Crewdson was born in Cornwall, England in 1809. Always delicate in health, toward the close of her life she was unable to leave her home. Most of her hymns were written during this period. She died in 1863. Her husband wrote of her: "As a constant sufferer, the spiritual life deepening and the intellectual life retaining all its power, she became well prepared to testify as to the all-sufficiency of her Saviour's love. Many felt that her sick room was the highest place to which they could resort for refreshment of spirit." **Key Verse:** The disciples asked each other, "What does he mean when he says, `You won't see me, and then you will see me'? And what does he mean when he says, `I am going to the Father'?" –John 16:17

◆ **33** ◆

BLESSED ASSURANCE
Blessed assurance, Jesus is mine!
O what a foretaste of glory divine!
Heir of salvation, purchase of God,
Born of His Spirit, washed in His blood.

> *Refrain*
> *This is my story, this is my song,*
> *Praising my Savior, all the day long;*
> *This is my story, this is my song,*
> *Praising my Savior, all the day long.*

Perfect submission, perfect delight,
Visions of rapture now burst on my sight;
Angels descending bring from above
Echoes of mercy, whispers of love. *Refrain*

Perfect submission, all is at rest
I in my Savior am happy and blest,

Watching and waiting, looking above,
Filled with His goodness, lost in His love. *Refrain*

About the writer: Fanny Crosby was the most prolific and perhaps the most popular writer of Sunday school hymns that America has ever produced. She was born in Putnam County, New York in 1820. When only six weeks old she lost her eyesight. Her first poem was written when she was eight. At the age of 15 she entered the Institution for the Blind in New York City, where she spent seven years as a pupil and 11 years (1847-1858) as a teacher. In 1844 she published a volume entitled *The Blind Girl and Other Poems*. In 1851 she accepted Christ and joined the Methodist Episcopal Church. In 1858 she married Alexander Van Alstyne, who was also, like herself, blind, had been a teacher in the Institution, and was possessed of rare musical talent. During her lifetime she wrote more than six thousand hymns. **Key Verses:** And since we have a great High Priest who rules over God's people, let us go right into the presence of God, with true hearts fully trusting him. For our evil consciences have been sprinkled with Christ's blood to make us clean, and our bodies have been washed with pure water. –Hebrews 10:21, 22

◆ 34 ◆

SHE LOVED HER SAVIOR
She loved her Savior, and to Him
Her costliest present brought;
To crown His head, or grace His Name,
No gift too rare she thought.

So let the Savior be adored,
And not the poor despised,
Give to the hungry from your hoard,
But all, give all to Christ.

Go, clothe the naked, lead the blind,
Give to the weary rest;
For sorrow's children comfort find,
And help for all distressed.

But give to Christ alone Thy heart,
Thy faith, Thy love supreme,
Then for His sake Thine alms impart,
And so give all to Him.

About the writer: William Cutter, an editor and publisher, was born in North Yarmouth, Maine in 1801. He was educated at Bowdoin College, where he was graduated in 1821. He wrote poetry and hymns as a hobby and his writings were contributed to the *Christian Mirror*, a periodical published in Portland. He died in 1867. **Key Verse:** After breakfast Jesus said to Simon Peter, "Simon son of John, do you love me more than these?"
"Yes, Lord," Peter replied, "you know I love you."
"Then feed my lambs," Jesus told him. –John 21:15

◆ **35** ◆

I SHALL NOT WANT
I shall not want: in deserts wild
Thou spread'st Thy table for Thy child;
While grace in streams for thirsting souls,
Thro' earth and Heaven forever rolls.

I shall not want: my darkest night
Thy loving smile shall fill with light;
While promises around me bloom,
And cheer me with divine perfume.

I shall not want: Thy righteousness
My soul shall clothe with glorious dress;
My blood-washed robe shall be more fair
Than garments kings or angels wear.

I shall not want: whate'er is good,
Of daily bread or angels' food,
Shall to my Father's child be sure,
So long as earth and Heaven endure.

About the writer: Charles Force Deems was a minister in the Methodist Episcopal Church, South. From 1866 until his death, in 1893, he was pastor of the Church of the Strangers, an independent congregation in New York City. In addition to being a pastor, he served as an agent of the American Bible Society, professor of Logic and Rhetoric at the University of North Carolina, and president of the Greensboro Female College, North Carolina. Deems was a popular preacher and forcible public speaker. As pastor to Commodore Vanderbilt he persuaded him to give a million dollars to the "Central University of the Methodist Episcopal Church, South" (now Vanderbilt University) in Nashville, Tennessee. **Key Verse:** The LORD is my shepherd; I have everything I need. –Psalm 23:1

◆ **36** ◆

COME UNTO ME, YE WEARY
"Come unto Me, ye weary, and I will give you rest."
O Blessed voice of Jesus, which comes to hearts oppressed!
It tells of benediction, of pardon, grace and peace,
Of joy that hath no ending, of love which cannot cease.

"Come unto Me, dear children, and I will give you light."
O loving voice of Jesus, which comes to cheer the night!
Our hearts are filled with sadness, and we had lost our way;
But He hath brought us gladness and songs at break of day.

"Come unto Me, ye fainting, and I will give you life."
O cheering voice of Jesus, which comes to aid our strife!
The foe is stern and eager, the fight is fierce and long;
But Thou hast made us mighty and stronger than the strong.

"And whosoever cometh I will not cast him out."
O welcome voice of Jesus, which drives away our doubt,
Which calls us, very sinners, unworthy though we be
Of love so free and boundless, to come, dear Lord, to Thee.

About the writer: William Chatterton Dix was born in Bristol, England in 1837. His entire career was spent working at a marine insurance company in Glasgow. During his lifetime, however, he published many books including *Hymns of Love and Joy*, 1861; *Altar Songs*, 1867; *Vision of All Saints*, 1871; and *Seekers of a City*, 1878. He died in 1898. **Key Verse:** Then Jesus said, "Come to me, all of you who are weary and carry heavy burdens, and I will give you rest." –Matthew 11:28

♦ 37 ♦

SOFTLY NOW THE LIGHT OF DAY
Softly now the light of day
Fades upon my sight away;
Free from care, from labor free,
Lord, I would commune with Thee.

Thou, Whose all pervading eye
Naught escapes, without, within,
Pardon each infirmity,
Open fault, and secret sin.

Soon for me the light of day
Shall forever pass away;
Then, from sin and sorrow free,
Take me, Lord, to dwell with Thee.

Thou Who, sinless, yet hast known
All of man's infirmity;
Then, from Thine eternal throne,
Jesus, look with pitying eye.

About the writer: George Washington Doane, a bishop in the Episcopal Church, was born in Trenton, New Jersey in 1799. He graduated from Union College in 1818 and entered the ministry in 1821. He served various churches until he was elected, in 1832, to the bishopric of New Jersey. A man of great energy, he founded Burlington College in 1846. His *Songs by the Way*, published when he was 25, gave evidence of unusual gifts as a poet and hymn writer.

Just after his death in 1859 his son published his complete works in four volumes. **Key Verse:** LORD, you have brought light to my life; my God, you light up my darkness. –Psalm 18:28

◆ 38 ◆

O HAPPY DAY, THAT FIXED MY CHOICE
O happy day, that fixed my choice
On Thee, my Savior and my God!
Well may this glowing heart rejoice,
And tell its raptures all abroad.

> *Refrain*
> *Happy day, happy day, when Jesus washed my sins away!*
> *He taught me how to watch and pray, and live rejoicing every day*
> *Happy day, happy day, when Jesus washed my sins away.*

O happy bond, that seals my vows
To Him Who merits all my love!
Let cheerful anthems fill His house,
While to that sacred shrine I move. *Refrain*

'Tis done: the great transaction's done!
I am the Lord's and He is mine;
He drew me, and I followed on;
Charmed to confess the voice divine. *Refrain*

High heaven, that heard the solemn vow,
That vow renewed shall daily hear,
Till in life's latest hour I bow
And bless in death a bond so dear. *Refrain*

About the writer: Philip Doddridge, one of the most distinguished Dissenting ministers of the eighteenth century, was the youngest of 20 children. He was born in 1702 and entered the ministry at the age of 19. In 1729 he moved to Northampton where he became pastor of the Dissenting Church and also organized and conducted a theological school for young preachers. As many as 150 students studied theology with him during the 20 years he was there.

His *Family Expositor* and *Rise and Progress of Religion in the Soul* were translated into many languages. He died of consumption in Lisbon, Portugal in 1751. It was his custom immediately after finishing a sermon to write a hymn embodying the doctrinal and devotional sentiment of the discourse. While this unique practice gives his hymns a doctrinal unity, they are typically suitable for one subject only, not for any occasion. **Key Verses:** Then they entered into a covenant to seek the LORD, the God of their ancestors, with all their heart and soul. They agreed that anyone who refused to seek the LORD, the God of Israel, would be put to death–whether young or old, man or woman. They shouted out their oath of loyalty to the LORD with trumpets blaring and horns sounding. –2 Chronicles 15:12-14

◆ 39 ◆

STAND UP, STAND UP FOR JESUS
Stand up, stand up for Jesus, ye soldiers of the cross;
Lift high His royal banner, it must not suffer loss.
From victory unto victory His army shall He lead,
Till every foe is vanquished, and Christ is Lord indeed.

Stand up, stand up for Jesus, the solemn watchword hear;
If while ye sleep He suffers, away with shame and fear;
Where'er ye meet with evil, within you or without,
Charge for the God of battles, and put the foe to rout.

Stand up, stand up for Jesus, the trumpet call obey;
Forth to the mighty conflict, in this His glorious day.
Ye that are brave now serve Him against unnumbered foes;
Let courage rise with danger, and strength to strength oppose.

Stand up, stand up for Jesus, the strife will not be long;
This day the noise of battle, the next the victor's song.
To those who vanquish evil a crown of life shall be;
They with the King of Glory shall reign eternally.

About the writer: George Duffield was born in Carlisle, Pennsylvania in 1818. He graduated from Union Theological Seminary in 1840 and was ordained an elder in the Presbyterian Church. He became a pastor of many of the leading Presbyterian Churches in the North and Northwest. He retired from the ministry in 1884 and settled in Detroit, Michigan. He died in 1888 in Bloomfield, New Jersey while on a visit to his son's widow. He was the author of many books about hymns including *English Hymns, Their Authors and History*, 1886, and *Latin Hymn Writers*, 1889. **Key Verses:** Put on all of God's armor so that you will be able to stand firm against all strategies and tricks of the Devil. For we are not fighting against people made of flesh and blood, but against the evil rulers and authorities of the unseen world, against those mighty powers of darkness who rule this world, and against wicked spirits in the heavenly realms. –Ephesians 6:11, 12

◆ **40** ◆

WHILE LIFE PROLONGS ITS PRECIOUS LIGHT
While life prolongs its precious light,
Mercy is found, and peace is given;
But soon, ah soon, approaching night
Shall blot out every hope of heaven.

While God invites, how blest the day!
How sweet the Gospel's charming sound!
Come sinners, haste, O haste away,
While yet a pardoning God is found.

Soon, borne on time's most rapid wing
Shall death command you to the grave,
Before His bar your spirits bring,
And none be found to hear or save.

And in that land of deep despair
No Sabbath's heavenly light shall rise,
No God regard your bitter prayer,
No Savior call you to the skies.

About the writer: Timothy Dwight, a distinguished Congregational minister and educator, was born in Northampton, Massachusetts in 1752. His mother was a daughter of Jonathan Edwards. He entered Yale College at the age of 13 and, graduating four years later, became a tutor; which position he resigned in 1777 to become chaplain in the Revolutionary army. He later became a pastor in Greenfield, Connecticut and, in 1795, was elected president of Yale College. He remained in this position until his death in 1817. He was the author of about a dozen hymns. **Key Verse:** Know this: A homeowner who knew exactly when a burglar was coming would not permit the house to be broken into. –Luke 12:39

◆ 41 ◆

THE LORD BE WITH US
The Lord be with us as we bend
His blessing to receive;
His gift of peace upon us send,
Before His courts we leave.

The Lord be with us as we walk
Along our homeward road;
In silent thought or friendly talk
Our hearts be near to God.

The Lord be with us as each day
His blessings we receive;
His gift of peace on all we pray,
Before His courts we leave.

The Lord be with us
   through the hours
Of slumber calm and deep,
Protect our homes,
   renew our powers,
And guard us while we sleep.

About the writer: John Ellerton, a clergyman of the Church of England, was born in London in 1826. He was educated at Trinity College, Cambridge, graduating in 1849. From 1850 until his death in 1893 he filled various positions in the Church of England as vicar and rector, being appointed Canon of St. Albans in 1892. He was the author of some prose writings, but is best known as a hymnologist. His contributions to hymnody are not numerous – about fifty original hymns and ten translations. **Key Verse:** The LORD who saved me from the claws of the lion and the bear will save me from this Philistine!" Saul finally consented. "All right, go ahead," he said. "And may the LORD be with you!" –1 Samuel 17:37

♦ 42 ♦

JUST AS I AM, WITHOUT ONE PLEA
Just as I am, without one plea,
But that Thy blood was shed for me,
And that Thou bidst me come to Thee,
O Lamb of God, I come, I come.

Just as I am, and waiting not
To rid my soul of one dark blot,
To Thee whose blood can cleanse each spot,
O Lamb of God, I come, I come.

Just as I am, though tossed about
With many a conflict, many a doubt,
Fightings and fears within, without,
O Lamb of God, I come, I come.

Just as I am, poor, wretched, blind;
Sight, riches, healing of the mind,
Yea, all I need in Thee to find,
O Lamb of God, I come, I come.

Just as I am, Thou wilt receive,
Wilt welcome, pardon, cleanse, relieve;
Because Thy promise I believe,
O Lamb of God, I come, I come.

Just as I am, of that free love
The breadth, length, depth, and height to prove,
Here for a season, then above,
O Lamb of God, I come, I come!

About the writer: Charlotte Elliott, the granddaughter of Henry Venn, an
eminent Church of England cleric, was born in 1789. She developed at quite
an early age a passion for music and art and she was unusually well educated

for her time. Sadly, from the age of 32 until her death in 1871, she was continually ill and bedridden. Despite this she wrote continuously throughout her lifetime, publishing several volumes. Her *Invalid's Hymn Book* was published in various editions from 1834 to 1854, and contained altogether one hundred and fifteen of her hymns. She shrank from publicity – nearly all her books and hymns were originally published anonymously. **Key Verse:** The next day John saw Jesus coming toward him and said, "Look! There is the Lamb of God who takes away the sin of the world!" –John 1:29

◆ **43** ◆

FAITH OF OUR FATHERS
Faith of our fathers, living still,
In spite of dungeon, fire and sword;
O how our hearts beat high with joy
Whenever we hear that glorious Word!
> *Refrain*
> *Faith of our fathers, holy faith!*
> *We will be true to thee till death.*

Faith of our fathers, we will strive
To win all nations unto Thee;
And through the truth that comes from God,
We all shall then be truly free. *Refrain*

Faith of our fathers, we will love
Both friend and foe in all our strife;
And preach Thee, too, as love knows how
By kindly words and virtuous life. *Refrain*

About the writer: Frederick William Faber was born in Yorkshire, England in 1814. He was educated at Harrow School and Balliol College, Oxford, which he entered in 1832. At Oxford he came under the influence of Catholic scholar John Henry Newman, then vicar of St. Mary's. He entered the ministry of the Church of England, taking deacon's orders in 1837 and priest's orders two years later. In 1845 he told his congregation that he could no longer remain in communion with the Church of England. The next day he was admitted into the Roman Catholic Church at Northampton. In 1849, he went to London and took charge of the Oratory of St. Philip Neri, where he remained until his death in 1863. In the preface to the 1849 edition of his hymns he wrote: "It seemed then in every way desirable that Catholics should have a hymn book for reading which should contain the mysteries of the faith in easy verse or different states of heart and conscience depicted with the same unadorned simplicity, for example, as the 'O for a closer walk with God' of the Olney Hymns." **Key Verses:** What is faith? It is the confident assurance that what we hope for is going to happen. It is the evidence of things we cannot yet see. God gave his approval to people in days of old because of their faith. –Hebrews 11:1, 2

◆ **44** ◆

IN THE FIELD WITH THEIR FLOCKS ABIDING

In the field with their flocks abiding,
They lay on the dewy ground;
And glimmering under the starlight,
The sheep lay white around;
When the light of the Lord streamed o'er them,
And lo! from heaven above,
An angel leaned from the glory,
And sang his song of love.
He sang, that first sweet Christmas,
The song that shall never cease.

> *Refrain*
> *"Glory to God in the highest,*
> *On earth good will and peace."*

"To you in the city of David
A Savior is born today!"
And sudden a host of the heavenly ones
Flashed forth to join the lay.
O never hath sweeter message
Thrilled home to the souls of men
And the heavens themselves had never heard
A gladder choir till then.
For they sang that Christmas carol

That never on earth shall cease. *Refrain*
And the shepherds came to the manger,
And gazed on the Holy Child;
And calmly o'er that rude cradle
The virgin mother smiled;
And the sky in the starlit silence,
Seemed full of the angel lay:
"To you in the City of David
A Savior is born today!"
O they sang, and we pray that never
The carol on earth shall cease. *Refrain*

About the writer: Frederick W. Farrar, a cleric in the Church of England, was the son of C. P. Farrar, a missionary to India. He was born in Bombay, India in 1831 and graduated from Trinity College, Cambridge with high honors in 1854. In 1876 he was made a Canon of Westminster Abbey and rector of St. Margaret's Church. Dr. Farrar became Dean of Canterbury in 1895 and died there in 1903. He was the author of many books including the best-seller *Life and Work of St. Paul.* **Key Verses:** That night some shepherds were in the fields outside the village, guarding their flocks of sheep. Suddenly, an angel of the Lord appeared among them, and the radiance of the Lord's glory surrounded them. They were terribly frightened. –Luke 2:8, 9

◆ **45** ◆

BLEST BE THE TIE THAT BINDS
Blest be the tie that binds
Our hearts in Christian love;
The fellowship of kindred minds
Is like to that above.

This glorious hope revives
Our courage by the way;
While each in expectation lives,
And longs to see the day.

Before our Father's throne
We pour our ardent prayers;
Our fears, our hopes, our aims,
Our comforts and our cares.

From sorrow, toil and pain,
And sin, we shall be free,
And perfect love and friendship reign
Through all eternity.

About the writer: John Fawcett was born in Yorkshire, England in 1739. He was converted under the preaching of George Whitefield and in 1765 became pastor of the Baptist Church at Wainsgate. He remained here until his death in 1817. He published many volumes on religious subjects throughout his life and wrote 166 hymns. Most of these hymns were composed especially to be sung at the conclusion of his sermons. **Key Verse:** I led Israel along with my ropes of kindness and love. I lifted the yoke from his neck, and I myself stooped to feed him. –Hosea 11:4

• **46** •

GREAT KING OF GLORY, COME
Great King of glory, come,
And with Thy favor crown
This temple as Thy home,
This people as Thine own;
Beneath this roof, O deign to show
How God can dwell with men below.

Here may Thine ears attend
Our interceding cries,
And grateful praise ascend,
Like incense, to the skies:
Here may Thy Word melodious sound,
And spread celestial joys around.

Here may our unborn sons
And daughters sound Thy praise,
And shine, like polished stones,
Through long succeeding days;
Here, Lord, display Thy saving power,
While temples stand and men adore.

Here may the listening throng
Receive Thy truth in love;
Here Christians join the song
Of seraphim above;
Till all, who humbly seek Thy face,
Rejoice in Thy abounding grace.

About the writer: Benjamin Francis, an English Baptist minister, was born in Wales in 1734. He joined the Baptist Church at 15 and began preaching when only 19. He accepted a call to the Baptist Church at Shortwood in 1757 and remained there until his death in 1799. An earnest and popular preacher, he received calls from London and elsewhere, but refused them all in deep devotion to his flock at Shortwood, He published several small volumes of poetry, among them two books of Welsh hymns. **Key Verse:** I heard a loud shout from the throne, saying, "Look, the home of God is now among his people! He will live with them, and they will be his people. God himself will be with them. –Revelation 21:3

◆ **47** ◆

GIVE TO THE WINDS THY FEARS
Give to the winds thy fears,
Hope and be undismayed.
God hears thy sighs and counts thy tears,
God shall lift up thy head.

Through waves and clouds and storms,
He gently clears thy way;
Wait thou His time; so shall this night
Soon end in joyous day.

Still heavy is thy heart?
Still sinks thy spirit down?
Cast off the world, let fear depart
Bid every care begone.

Thou seest our weakness, Lord;
Our hearts are known to Thee;
O lift Thou up the sinking hand,
Confirm the feeble knee!

Let us in life, in death,
Thy steadfast truth declare,

And publish with our latest breath
Thy love and guardian care.

About the writer: Paul Gerhardt, a distinguished Lutheran minister, and, next to Luther, the most popular hymn writer of Germany, was born in Saxony in 1607. He studied at the University of Wittenberg and later became a tutor in the family of his sponsor Andreas Barthold; whose daughter he later married in 1655. In the meantime he had begun to preach and was ordained as chief pastor at Mittenwalde, near Berlin. Several of his hymns were published in 1653 in the *Berlin Hymn Book*. In 1669 he was appointed archdeacon of Lubben in Saxony where he died in 1676. **Key Verse:** I prayed to the LORD, and he answered me, freeing me from all my fears. –Psalm 34:4

◆ **48** ◆

HE LEADETH ME
He leadeth me, O Blessed thought!
O words with heav'nly comfort fraught!
Whate'er I do, where'er I be
Still 'tis God's hand that leadeth me.
> *Refrain*
> *He leadeth me, He leadeth me,*
> *By His own hand He leadeth me;*
> *His faithful follower I would be,*
> *For by His hand He leadeth me.*

Sometimes mid scenes of deepest gloom,
Sometimes where Eden's bowers bloom,
By waters still, over troubled sea,
Still 'tis His hand that leadeth me. *Refrain*

Lord, I would place my hand in Thine,
Nor ever murmur nor repine;
Content, whatever lot I see,
Since 'tis my God that leadeth me. *Refrain*

And when my task on earth is done,
When by Thy grace the vict'ry's won,
E'en death's cold wave I will not flee,
Since God through Jordan leadeth me. *Refrain*

About the writer: Joseph Henry Gilmore, a Baptist minister, was born in Boston in 1834. He entered Brown University in 1854 and graduated with high honors in 1858. That same year he entered Newton Theological Seminary, graduating in 1861. He was ordained in 1862 as pastor of a Baptist Church in Fisherville, New Hampshire. In 1868 he became professor of logic and English literature at the University of Rochester, a position he held until his death. He wrote many scholarly works, including *Outlines of English and American Literature*, 1905, and a number of hymns. **Key Verses:** The LORD is my shepherd; I have everything I need. He lets me rest in green meadows; he leads me beside peaceful streams. He renews my strength. He guides me along right paths, bringing honor to his name. –Psalm 23:1-3

◆ 49 ◆

O WORSHIP THE KING
O worship the King, all glorious above,
O gratefully sing His power and His love;
Our Shield and Defender, the Ancient of Days,
Pavilioned in splendor, and girded with praise.

O tell of His might, O sing of His grace,
Whose robe is the light, Whose canopy space,
His chariots of wrath the deep thunderclouds form,
And dark is His path on the wings of the storm.

The earth with its store of wonders untold,
Almighty, Thy power hath founded of old;
Established it fast by a changeless decree,
And round it hath cast, like a mantle, the sea.

Thy bountiful care, what tongue can recite?
It breathes in the air, it shines in the light;

It streams from the hills, it descends to the plain,
And sweetly distills in the dew and the rain.

O measureless might! Ineffable love!
While angels delight to worship Thee above,
The humbler creation, though feeble their lays,
With true adoration shall all sing Thy praise.

About the writer: Robert Grant was born in India in 1785. His father was
a leading officer of the East India Company. He graduated from Cambridge in
1804 and was admitted to the bar in 1807. He later was appointed Governor
of Bombay in 1824. He died in India in 1838. He was the author of several
volumes on the work of the East India Company and also of 12 hymns;
which his brother, Lord Glenelg, published the year after his death. "O
Worship the King" is considered by many to be one of the greatest hymns
ever written. **Key Verses:** Praise the LORD, I tell myself; O LORD my
God, how great you are! You are robed with honor and with majesty; you are
dressed in a robe of light. You stretch out the starry curtain of the heavens.
–Psalm 104:1, 2

◆ **50** ◆

JESUS, AND SHALL IT EVER BE
Jesus, and shall it ever be,
A mortal man, ashamed of Thee?
Ashamed of Thee, whom angels praise,
Whose glories shine through endless days?

Ashamed of Jesus! sooner far
Let night disown each radiant star!
'Tis midnight with my soul, till He,
Bright Morning Star, bid darkness flee.

Ashamed of Jesus! O as soon
Let morning blush to own the sun!
He sheds the beams of light divine
O'er this benighted soul of mine.

Ashamed of Jesus! that dear Friend
On Whom my hopes of Heav'n depend!
No; when I blush, be this my shame,
That I no more revere His Name.

Ashamed of Jesus! yes, I may
When I've no guilt to wash away;
No tear to wipe, no good to crave,
No fears to quell, no soul to save.

Ashamed of Jesus! empty pride!
I'll boast a Savior crucified,
And O may this my portion be,
My Savior not ashamed of me!

About the writer: Joseph Grigg, an English Presbyterian minister, was born in 1720. He began writing hymns when he was only ten years old. He entered the ministry in 1743 and became an assistant pastor at the Silver Street Presbyterian Church, London. He continued here only four years when he married and settled in St. Albans. He retired from the active work of the ministry at this time and began writing. His published works eventually numbered about forty devotional and scholarly volumes. He died in 1768. In 1806 his hymns were collected and published. **Key Verse:** If a person is ashamed of me and my message in these adulterous and sinful days, I, the Son of Man, will be ashamed of that person when I return in the glory of my Father with the holy angels. –Mark 8:38

❖ **51** ❖

I LOVE TO TELL THE STORY

I love to tell the story of unseen things above,
Of Jesus and His glory, of Jesus and His love.
I love to tell the story, because I know 'tis true;
It satisfies my longings as nothing else can do.

Refrain
I love to tell the story, 'twill be my theme in glory,
To tell the old, old story of Jesus and His love.

I love to tell the story; more wonderful it seems
Than all the golden fancies of all our golden dreams.
I love to tell the story, it did so much for me;
And that is just the reason I tell it now to thee. *Refrain*

I love to tell the story; 'tis pleasant to repeat
What seems, each time I tell it, more wonderfully sweet.
I love to tell the story, for some have never heard
The message of salvation from God's own holy Word. *Refrain*

I love to tell the story, for those who know it best
Seem hungering and thirsting to hear it like the rest.
And when, in scenes of glory, I sing the new, new song,
'Twill be the old, old story that I have loved so long. *Refrain*

About the writer: Katherine Hankey is the author of two of the world's most popular hymns, both with similar themes: "The Old, Old Story" and "I Love to Tell the Story." The daughter of an English banker she dedicated her life to writing and publishing devotional verse. **Key Verse:** Come and listen, all you who fear God, and I will tell you what he did for me. –Psalm 66:16

◆ 52 ◆

COME, YE SINNERS, POOR AND NEEDY
Come, ye sinners, poor and needy,
Weak and wounded, sick and sore;
Jesus ready stands to save you,
Full of pity, love and power.
> *Refrain*
> *I will arise and go to Jesus,*
> *He will embrace me in His arms;*
> *In the arms of my dear Savior,*
> *O there are ten thousand charms.*

Come, ye thirsty, come, and welcome,
God's free bounty glorify;

True belief and true repentance,
Every grace that brings you nigh. *Refrain*

View Him prostrate in the garden;
On the ground your Maker lies.
On the bloody tree behold Him;
Sinner, will this not suffice? *Refrain*

Let not conscience make you linger,
Not of fitness fondly dream;
All the fitness He requireth
Is to feel your need of Him. *Refrain*

About the writer: Joseph Hart, a Congregational minister in England, was born in 1712 of pious parents. He was well educated and was for many years a teacher of the classics. As a young man he renounced religion but, at the age of 40, began reading the Bible and found the peace he sought. Many of his best hymns were written within the next two years following his conversion. His *Hymns Composed on Various Subjects, with the Author's Experience* was published in several editions during his lifetime. At 48 he became the pastor of an Independent congregation in London, a position he held until his death in 1768. His funeral was attended by 20,000 people. **Key Verses:** Then Jesus said, "Come to me, all of you who are weary and carry heavy burdens, and I will give you rest. Take my yoke upon you. Let me teach you, because I am humble and gentle, and you will find rest for your souls. For my yoke fits perfectly, and the burden I give you is light." –Matthew 11:28-30

◆ 53 ◆
GENTLY LORD, O GENTLY LEAD US
Gently Lord, O gently lead us,
Pilgrims in this vale of tears,
Through the trials yet decreed us,
Till our last great change appears.
When temptation's darts assail us,
When in devious paths we stray,

Let Thy goodness never fail us,
Lead us in Thy perfect way.

In the hour of pain and anguish,
In the hour when death draws near,
Suffer not our hearts to languish,
Suffer not our souls to fear;
And, when mortal life is ended,
Bid us in Thine arms to rest,
Till, by angel bands attended,
We awake among the blest.

About the writer: Thomas Hastings was born in Washington, Connecticut in 1784. He edited and largely contributed to *Spiritual Songs*, 1832; *Christian Psalmist*, 1836; *The Mother's Hymn Book*, 1849; and *Devotional Hymns and Religious Poems*, 1850. He was also the editor of a number of music books. He died in New York City in 1872. "His aim," wrote a contemporary, "was the greater glory of God through better musical worship; and to this end he was always training choirs, compiling works, and composing music." **Key Verse:** And forgive us our sins–just as we forgive those who have sinned against us. And don't let us yield to temptation. –Luke 11:4

◆ **54** ◆

BREATHE ON ME, BREATH OF GOD
Breathe on me, breath of God,
Fill me with life anew,
That I may love what Thou dost love,
And do what Thou wouldst do.

Breathe on me, breath of God,
Until my heart is pure,
Until with Thee I will one will,
To do and to endure.

Breathe on me, breath of God,
Blend all my soul with Thine,

Until this earthly part of me
Glows with Thy fire divine.

Breathe on me, breath of God,
So shall I never die,
But live with Thee the perfect life
Of Thine eternity.

About the writer: Edwin Hatch, a Church of England clergyman, was born in Derby, England in 1835. He graduated from Oxford in 1857 and became, in 1867, vice principal of St. Mary's Hall, Oxford. He was rector of Purleigh from 1883 until his death in 1889. His hymns and other poems were published in a posthumous volume titled *Towards Fields of Light*, 1890. **Key Verse:** Then he breathed on them and said to them, "Receive the Holy Spirit." – John 20:22

◆ **55** ◆

TAKE MY LIFE AND LET IT BE
Take my life, and let it be consecrated, Lord, to Thee.
Take my moments and my days; let them flow in ceaseless praise.
Take my hands, and let them move at the impulse of Thy love.
Take my feet, and let them be swift and beautiful for Thee.

Take my voice, and let me sing always, only, for my King.
Take my lips, and let them be filled with messages from Thee.
Take my silver and my gold; not a mite would I withhold.
Take my intellect, and use every power as Thou shalt choose.

Take my will, and make it Thine; it shall be no longer mine.
Take my heart, it is Thine own; it shall be Thy royal throne.
Take my love, my Lord, I pour at Thy feet its treasure store.
Take myself, and I will be ever, only, all for Thee.

About the writer: Frances Ridley Havergal was born in Worcestershire, England in 1836. "When fifteen years old," she once wrote, "I committed my soul to the Saviour, and earth and heaven seemed brighter from that moment." Highly educated, her knowledge of Hebrew and Greek and modern languages was extensive and her hymn writing skills are celebrated to this day. She died in 1879 but her popularity and influence as an author and hymn writer have increased since her death. About seventy-five of her hymns are in common use. **Key Verse:** And so, dear brothers and sisters, I plead with you to give your bodies to God. Let them be a living and holy sacrifice–the kind he will accept. When you think of what he has done for you, is this too much to ask? –Romans 12:1

◆ **56** ◆

I NEED THEE EVERY HOUR
I need Thee every hour, most gracious Lord;
No tender voice like Thine can peace afford.

> *Refrain*
> *I need Thee, O I need Thee;*
> *Every hour I need Thee;*
> *O bless me now, my Savior,*
> *I come to Thee.*

I need Thee every hour, stay Thou nearby;
Temptations lose their power when Thou art nigh. *Refrain*

I need Thee every hour, in joy or pain;
Come quickly and abide, or life is in vain. *Refrain*

I need Thee every hour, most Holy One;
O make me Thine indeed, Thou Blessed Son. *Refrain*

About the writer: Annie Sherwood Hawks was born in Hoosick, New York in 1835. She resided in Brooklyn until her death. It was here that she wrote her best known hymn, "I Need Thee Every Hour" in 1872. **Key Verse:** So let us come boldly to the throne of our gracious God. There we will receive his mercy, and we will find grace to help us when we need it. –Hebrews 4:16

✦ 57 ✦

WE HOPE IN THEE, O GOD!

We hope in Thee, O God!
The day wears on to night;
Thick shadows lie across our world,
In Thee alone is light.

We hope in Thee, O God!
Our joys go one by one,
But lonely hearts can rest in Thee,
When all beside is gone.

We hope in Thee, O God!
Hope fails us otherwhere;
But since Thou art in all that is,
Peace takes the hand of care.

We hope in Thee, O God!
In Whom none hope in vain;
We cling to Thee in love and trust,
And joy succeeds to pain.

About the writer: Marianne Hearn was born in Kent, England in 1834. She was a member of the Baptist Church and was on the editorial staff of that denomination's religious periodical *Christian World*. At her death in 1909 she was called "one of the most honored women in the Baptist Church in England." **Key Verse:** Let your unfailing love surround us, LORD, for our hope is in you alone. –Psalm 33:22

✦ 58 ✦

HOLY, HOLY, HOLY

Holy, holy, holy! Lord God Almighty!
Early in the morning our song shall rise to Thee;
Holy, holy, holy, merciful and mighty!
God in three Persons, Blessed Trinity!

Holy, holy, holy! All the saints adore Thee,
Casting down their golden crowns around the glassy sea;
Cherubim and seraphim falling down before Thee,
Who was, and is, and evermore shall be.

Holy, holy, holy! though the darkness hide Thee,
Though the eye of sinful man Thy glory may not see;
Only Thou art holy; there is none beside Thee,
Perfect in power, in love, and purity.

Holy, holy, holy! Lord God Almighty!
All Thy works shall praise Thy Name, in earth, and sky, and sea;
Holy, holy, holy; merciful and mighty!
God in three Persons, Blessed Trinity!

About the writer: Reginald Heber, a bishop of the Church of England, was born in Malpas, England in 1783. He was educated at Brasenose College, Oxford, where he early took the prize for both Latin and English poems. Ordained in 1807 he became the Missionary Bishop of Calcutta from 1823 until his death in 1826. His hymns were collected and published the year after his death under the title *Hymns Written and Adapted to the Weekly Church Service of the Year.* **Key Verse:** In a great chorus they sang, "Holy, holy, holy is the LORD Almighty! The whole earth is filled with his glory!" –Isaiah 6:3

◆ **59** ◆

THERE'S A SONG IN THE AIR
There's a song in the air! There's a star in the sky!
There's a mother's deep prayer and a baby's low cry!
And the star rains its fire while the beautiful sing,
For the manger of Bethlehem cradles a King!

There's a tumult of joy o'er the wonderful birth,
For the virgin's sweet Boy is the Lord of the earth.
Ay! the star rains its fire while the beautiful sing,
For the manger of Bethlehem cradles a King!

In the light of that star lie the ages impearled;
And that song from afar has swept over the world.
Every hearth is aflame, and the beautiful sing
In the homes of the nations that Jesus is King!

We rejoice in the light, and we echo the song
That comes down through the night from the heavenly throng.
Ay! we shout to the lovely evangel they bring,
And we greet in His cradle our Savior and King!

About the writer: Josiah Gilbert Holland was born in Belchertown, Massachusetts in 1819. He was a farmer's son who had few chances for public education. Yet he succeeded in attending a high school at Northampton for a time and, at the age of 21, he began the study of medicine; graduating with a degree from Berkshire Medical College in 1844. He disliked medicine, however, and became a writer. In 1870 he founded *Scribner's Monthly* and was its editor until his death in 1881. He wrote a popular collection of hymns that included his best known work, "There's A Song In the Air." **Key Verse:** She gave birth to her first child, a son. She wrapped him snugly in strips of cloth and laid him in a manger, because there was no room for them in the village inn. –Luke 2:7

✦ 60 ✦

O JESUS, THOU ART STANDING

O Jesus, Thou art standing, outside the fast closed door,
In lowly patience waiting to pass the threshold o'er:
Shame on us, Christian brothers, His Name and sign who bear,
O shame, thrice shame upon us, to keep Him standing there!

O Jesus, Thou art knocking; and lo, that hand is scarred,
And thorns Thy brow encircle, and tears Thy face have marred:
O love that passeth knowledge, so patiently to wait!
O sin that hath no equal, so fast to bar the gate!

O Jesus, Thou art pleading in accents meek and low,
"I died for you, My children, and will you treat Me so?"
O Lord, with shame and sorrow we open now the door;
Dear Savior, enter, enter, and leave us nevermore.

About the writer: William Walsham How, a bishop of the Church of England, was born in Shrewsbury, England in 1823. He graduated from Oxford in 1845 and was ordained to the ministry in 1846. He held various positions in the Church of England before he became bishop in 1888. He died in 1897. He compiled *Psalms and Hymns*, 1854, and contributed several hymns to *Church Hymns*, 1871. Bishop How's hymns are characterized by a simplicity of manner and a warmth of feeling that have made some of them very popular.

Key Verse: Look! Here I stand at the door and knock. If you hear me calling and open the door, I will come in, and we will share a meal as friends. – Revelation 3:20

◆ **61** ◆

I'M GOING HOME

My heav'nly home is bright and fair,
Nor pain nor death can enter there;
Its glitt'ring towers the sun outshine,
That heav'nly mansion shall be mine.

> *Refrain*
> *I'm going home, I'm going home,*
> *I'm going home to die no more,*
> *To die no more, to die no more,*
> *I'm going home to die no more.*

My Father's home is built on high,
Far, far above the starry sky;
When from this earthly prison free,
That heav'nly mansion mine shall be. *Refrain*

Let others seek a home below,
Which flames devour, or waves o'erflow;
Be mine a happier lot to own
A heav'nly mansion near the throne. *Refrain*

About the writer: William Hunter, a minister in the Methodist Episcopal Church, was born in Ireland in 1811 but came to America as a child. He graduated from Madison College in 1833 and was for a number of years professor of Hebrew and Biblical Literature at Alleghany College. He was editor of the *Pittsburg Christian Advocate* from 1844 to 1852 and was the author of a large number of hymns, which he published in his *Select Melodies* (1838-1851) and *Songs of Devotion* (1860). He died in 1877. **Key Verse:** There are many rooms in my Father's home, and I am going to prepare a place for you. If this were not so, I would tell you plainly. –John 14:2

• 62 •

NEW EVERY MORNING IS THE LOVE

New every morning is the love
Our wakening and uprising prove;
Through sleep and darkness safely brought,
Restored to life and power and thought.

New mercies, each returning day,
Hover around us while we pray;
New perils past, new sins forgiven,
New thoughts of God, new hopes of heaven.

If, on our daily course, our mind
Be set to hallow all we find,
New treasures still, of countless price,
God will provide for sacrifice.

Seek we no more; content with these,
Let present rapture, comfort, ease—
As heaven shall bid them, come and go:
The secret this of rest below.

Only, O Lord, in Thy dear love,
Fit us for perfect rest above,
And help us, this and every day,
To live more nearly as we pray.

About the writer: John Keble was born in 1792 and graduated from Oxford in 1810. He was ordained in 1815. In 1827 he published his well-known volume, *The Christian Year*; ninety-six editions of which appeared before his death. A sermon preached by him on "National Apostasy" is regarded as the origin of the tractarian movement in 1833. He wrote eight of the "Tracts for the Times." He was the author of several volumes of hymns including *A Metrical Version of the Psalms*, 1839, and *Lyra Innocentium*, 1846. He died in 1866. **Key Verses:** The unfailing love of the LORD never ends! By his mercies we have been kept from complete destruction. Great is his faithfulness; his mercies begin afresh each day. —Lamentations 3:22, 23

◆ 63 ◆

HOW FIRM A FOUNDATION
How firm a foundation, ye saints of the Lord,
Is laid for your faith in His excellent Word!
What more can He say than to you He hath said,
You, who unto Jesus for refuge have fled?

In every condition, in sickness, in health;
In poverty's vale, or abounding in wealth;
At home and abroad, on the land, on the sea,
As thy days may demand, shall thy strength ever be.

Fear not, I am with thee, O be not dismayed,
For I am thy God and will still give thee aid;
I'll strengthen and help thee, and cause thee to stand
Upheld by My righteous, omnipotent hand.

When through fiery trials thy pathways shall lie,
My grace, all sufficient, shall be thy supply;
The flame shall not hurt thee; I only design
Thy dross to consume, and thy gold to refine.

The soul that on Jesus has leaned for repose,
I will not, I will not desert to its foes;
That soul, though all hell should endeavor to shake,
I'll never, no never, no never forsake.

About the writer: Not much is known for certain about the author of this hymn. Variously attributed to John Keene, R. Keen, or George Keith, it is believed that the writer was a song leader in the Baptist Church in London in the late 18th century. This is because John Rippon (1751-1836) was the pastor of this church when his volume titled *A Selection of Hymns from the Best Authors*, 1787, included "How Firm a Foundation." The composer was

listed as R. Keen. Later volumes gave different credit so the mystery remains.
Key Verse: Stay away from the love of money; be satisfied with what you
have. For God has said, "I will never fail you. I will never forsake you."
–Hebrews 13:5

◆ 64 ◆

HARK, TEN THOUSAND HARPS AND VOICES

Hark, ten thousand harps and voices
Sound the note of praise above!
Jesus reigns, and Heav'n rejoices,
Jesus reigns, the God of love;
See, He sits on yonder throne;
Jesus rules the world alone.
>   *Refrain*
>   *Hallelujah! Hallelujah! Hallelujah! Amen!*

Jesus, hail! Whose glory brightens
All above, and gives it worth;
Lord of life, Thy smile enlightens,
Cheers, and charms Thy saints on earth;
When we think of love like Thine,
Lord, we own it love divine. *Refrain*

King of glory, reign forever!
Thine an everlasting crown.
Nothing from Thy love shall sever
Those whom Thou hast made Thine own:
Happy objects of Thy grace,
Destined to behold Thy face. *Refrain*

Savior, hasten Thine appearing;
Bring, O bring the glorious day,
When, the awful summons bearing,
Heaven and earth shall pass away;
Then with golden harps we'll sing,
"Glory, glory to our King!" *Refrain*

About the writer: Thomas Kelly was born in Dublin, Ireland in 1769. He graduated from Trinity College, Dublin University and entered the ministry of the Established Church. His evangelical preaching proved too strong for the Established Church and he was forbidden by Archbishop Fowler to preach in the city. He became an Independent and preached in various Dublin locations for more than sixty years. He died in 1854. His *Scripture Hymns* grew from a volume of 96 hymns, first published in 1804, to a collection of 765 in 1853. All were original. **Key Verse:** Then I looked again, and I heard the singing of thousands and millions of angels around the throne and the living beings and the elders. –Revelation 5:11

◆ **65** ◆

PRAISE GOD, FROM WHOM ALL BLESSINGS FLOW (DOXOLOGY)
Praise God, from Whom all blessings flow;
Praise Him, all creatures here below;
Praise Him above, ye heavenly host;
Praise Father, Son, and Holy Ghost.

About the writer: Thomas Ken, a bishop of the Church of England, was born in Berkhampstead, England in 1637. He was educated at Winchester School and Oxford University, graduating in 1661. With six other bishops he refused to publish the "Declaration of Indulgence" issued by James II in 1688 and was imprisoned in the Tower of London. After his release he spent the rest of his life writing hymns and devotional works. He died in 1711. **Key Verse:** Whatever is good and perfect comes to us from God above, who created all heaven's lights. Unlike them, he never changes or casts shifting shadows. –James 1:17

◆ **66** ◆

BREAK THOU THE BREAD OF LIFE
Break Thou the bread of life, dear Lord, to me,
As Thou didst break the loaves beside the sea;
Beyond the sacred page I seek Thee, Lord;
My spirit pants for Thee, O living Word!

Bless Thou the truth, dear Lord, to me, to me,
As Thou didst bless the bread by Galilee;
Then shall all bondage cease, all fetters fall;
And I shall find my peace, my all in all.

Thou art the bread of life, O Lord, to me,
Thy holy Word the truth that saveth me;
Give me to eat and live with Thee above;
Teach me to love Thy truth, for Thou art love.

O send Thy Spirit, Lord, now unto me,
That He may touch my eyes, and make me see:
Show me the truth concealed within Thy Word,
And in Thy Book revealed I see the Lord.

About the writer: Mary Artemisia Lathbury was born in Manchester, New York in 1841. After graduating from school she became an art teacher and later engaged in editorial work. She contributed a number of hymns to the *Methodist Hymnal*; including her best known work, "Break Thou the Bread of Life." **Key Verse:** Jesus replied, "I am the bread of life. No one who comes to me will ever be hungry again. Those who believe in me will never thirst." –John 6:35

♦ 67 ♦

A MIGHTY FORTRESS IS OUR GOD
A mighty fortress is our God, a bulwark never failing;
Our helper He, amid the flood of mortal ills prevailing:
For still our ancient foe doth seek to work us woe;
His craft and power are great, and, armed with cruel hate,
On earth is not his equal.

Did we in our own strength confide, our striving would be losing;
Were not the right Man on our side, the Man of God's own choosing:
Dost ask who that may be? Christ Jesus, it is He;
Lord Sabbath, His Name, from age to age the same,
And He must win the battle.

And though this world, with devils filled, should threaten to undo us,
We will not fear, for God hath willed His truth to triumph through us:
The Prince of Darkness grim, we tremble not for him;
His rage we can endure, for lo, his doom is sure,
One little word shall fell him.

That word above all earthly powers, no thanks to them, abideth;
The Spirit and the gifts are ours through Him Who with us sideth:
Let goods and kindred go, this mortal life also;
The body they may kill: God's truth abideth still,
His kingdom is forever.

About the writer: Martin Luther, the hero of the Reformation, was born in the village of Eisleben in 1483. He entered the University at Erfurt in 1501 and graduated with honors. In 1505 he entered an Augustinian monastery at Erfurt and was consecrated to the priesthood in 1507. He was a diligent scholar and in 1508 was called to the chair of Philosophy at the University of Wittenberg. In 1512 he received the degree of Doctor of Theology. In the meantime he made a pilgrimage to Rome where he saw much corruption among the clergy; but still his faith was strong in the Roman Church. It was the shameless sale of indulgences by Tetzel, authorized by Leo X, that first opened his eyes and determined him to make public opposition. On October 31, 1517, at midday, Luther posted his ninety-five Theses against the Merits of Indulgences on the church door at Wittenberg. That day was the birthday of the Reformation. The burning of the pope's bull of excommunication in 1520, the Diet of Worms in 1521, Luther's concealment in the castle at Wartburg, and his marriage in 1525 are just a few events in his epic life. It was during his Wartburg captivity that he translated the New Testament, published in 1522, into the mother tongue of the German people. After giving them the Scriptures he felt the need for psalms and hymns in the German language. The first collection of Luther's hymns was published in 1524. He died in 1546. **Key Verse:** God is our refuge and strength, always ready to help in times of trouble. –Psalm 46:1

◆ 68 ◆

GRACIOUS SPIRIT, DWELL WITH ME

Gracious Spirit, dwell with me!
I myself would gracious be;
And with words that help and heal
Would Thy life in mine reveal;
And with actions bold and meek
Would for Christ my Savior speak.

Mighty Spirit, dwell with me!
I myself would mighty be;
Mighty so as to prevail,
Where unaided man must fail;
Ever, by a mighty hope,
Pressing on and bearing up.

Truthful Spirit, dwell with me!
I myself would truthful be;
And with wisdom kind and clear
Let Thy life in mine appear;
And with actions brotherly
Speak my Lord's sincerity.

Holy Spirit, dwell with me!
I myself would holy be;
Separate from sin, I would
Choose and cherish all things good,
And whatever I can be
Give to Him Who gave me Thee!

About the writer: Thomas Toke Lynch, an English Congregational minister, was born in Essex, England in 1818. He was pastor of a small church at Highgate until illness forced his retirement for three years (1856-1859). He resumed pastoral relations in 1860 with his former parishioners – who completed a new place of worship (Mornington Church) on Hampstead Road, London in 1862. Here he continued to preach until his death in 1871. His hymns were published in a volume titled *The Rivulet, a Contribution to Sacred Song*, which appeared in several editions from 1855-1868. **Key Verse:** Peter replied, "Each of you must turn from your sins and turn to God, and be baptized in the name of Jesus Christ for the forgiveness of your sins. Then you will receive the gift of the Holy Spirit." –Acts 2:38

◆ 69 ◆

ABIDE WITH ME

Abide with me; fast falls the eventide;
The darkness deepens; Lord with me abide.
When other helpers fail and comforts flee,
Help of the helpless, O abide with me.

Swift to its close ebbs out life's little day;
Earth's joys grow dim; its glories pass away;
Change and decay in all around I see;
O Thou who changest not, abide with me.

I need Thy presence every passing hour.
What but Thy grace can foil the tempter's power?
Who, like Thyself, my guide and stay can be?
Through cloud and sunshine, Lord, abide with me.

I fear no foe, with Thee at hand to bless;
Ills have no weight, and tears no bitterness.
Where is death's sting? Where, grave, thy victory?
I triumph still, if Thou abide with me.

Hold Thou Thy cross before my closing eyes;
Shine through the gloom and point me to the skies.
Heaven's morning breaks, and earth's vain shadows flee;
In life, in death, O Lord, abide with me.

About the writer: Henry Francis Lyte, a clergyman in the Church of England, was born in Kelso, Scotland in 1793. He was educated at Trinity College, Dublin where he graduated in 1814. During his college career he won the prize for the best English poem on three occasions. In 1818 he experienced a great spiritual change which influenced the rest of his life. He came to know a fellow minister who was sick but who died happy, trusting alone in the atonement and power of his Savior. Lyte wrote concerning himself: "I was greatly affected by the whole matter, and brought to look at life and its issue with a different eye than before; and I began to study my Bible and preach in another manner than I had previously done." The last hymn he wrote, "Abide with me," is his best known. **Key Verses:** By this time they were nearing Emmaus and the end of their journey. Jesus would have gone on, but they begged him to stay the night with them, since it was getting late. So he went home with them. –Luke 24:28, 29

♦ 70 ♦

O LOVE THAT WILT NOT LET ME GO

O Love that wilt not let me go,
I rest my weary soul in thee;
I give thee back the life I owe,
That in thine ocean depths its flow
May richer, fuller be.

O Joy that seekest me through pain,
I cannot close my heart to thee;
I trace the rainbow through the rain,
And feel the promise is not vain,
That morn shall tearless be.

O light that followest all my way,
I yield my flickering torch to thee;
My heart restores its borrowed ray,
That in thy sunshine's blaze its day
May brighter, fairer be.

O Cross that liftest up my head,
I dare not ask to fly from thee;
I lay in dust life's glory dead,
And from the ground there
          blossoms red
Life that shall endless be.

About the writer: George Matheson, a minister in the Church of Scotland, was born in Glasgow, Scotland in 1842. He entered Glasgow University in 1857, spending five years in the arts and four years in the study of Divinity. He was licensed to preach in 1866. Matheson was entirely blind during the greater portion of his life. While in school he had to depend upon the sight of others. He died in 1906. Of the 25 books he wrote, one was a hymnal titled *Sacred Songs*, 1890. **Key Verse:** But I trust in your unfailing love. I will rejoice because you have rescued me. –Psalm 13:5

♦ 71 ♦

I AM COMING TO THE CROSS

I am coming to the cross;
I am poor and weak and blind;
I am counting all but dross;
I shall full salvation find.
    Refrain
    I am trusting, Lord, in Thee.
    Blessed Lamb of Calvary;
    Humbly at Thy cross I bow.
    Save me, Jesus, save me now.

Long my heart has sighed for Thee;
Long has evil reigned within;
Jesus sweetly speaks to me:
"I will cleanse you from all sin."
Refrain

Here I give my all to Thee:
Friends and time and earthly store;
Soul and body Thine to be,
Wholly Thine forevermore. *Refrain*

Jesus comes! He fills my soul!
Perfected in Him I am;
I am every whit made whole:
Glory, glory to the Lamb! *Refrain*

About the writer: William McDonald, a minister in the Methodist Episcopal
Church, was born in Belmont, Maine in 1820. He served various pastoral
charges in the North and West and was, for several years, the editor of the
Christian Witness. From 1870 until his death he did much evangelistic work.
He was the publisher of several small volumes of hymns for social worship.
He died in 1901. **Key Verse:** I myself no longer live, but Christ lives in me.
So I live my life in this earthly body by trusting in the Son of God, who loved
me and gave himself for me. –Galatians 2:20

♦ 72 ♦

I KNOW THAT MY REDEEMER LIVES

I know that my Redeemer lives;
What comfort this sweet sentence gives!
He lives, He lives, who once was dead;
He lives, my ever living Head.

He lives to bless me with His love,
He lives to plead for me above.
He lives my hungry soul to feed,
He lives to help in time of need.

He lives triumphant from the grave,
He lives eternally to save,
He lives all glorious in the sky,
He lives exalted there on high.

He lives and grants me daily breath;
He lives, and I shall conquer death:
He lives my mansion to prepare;
He lives to bring me safely there.

He lives, all glory to His Name!
He lives, my Jesus, still the same.
Oh, the sweet joy this sentence gives,
I know that my Redeemer lives!

About the writer: Samuel Medley, a Baptist minister, was born in
Hertfordshire, England in 1738. He joined the navy and was severely wounded.
During his recovery someone read to him a sermon by Dr. Isaac Watts, which
led to his conversion. After his recovery he entered the ministry. For the last
27 years of his life he was the influential pastor of a large Baptist Church in
Liverpool. He died in 1799. His hymns, 230 in number, were collected and
published the following year under the title of *Medley's Hymns*. A biographer
wrote, "The charm of *Medley's Hymns* consists less in their poetry than in
the warmth and occasional pathos with which they give expression to the
Christian experience." **Key Verse:** But as for me, I know that my Redeemer
lives, and that he will stand upon the earth at last. –Job 19:25

◆ 73 ◆

THERE'S A FRIEND FOR LITTLE CHILDREN
There's a Friend for little children
Above the bright blue sky,
A Friend who never changes,
Whose love will never die;
Our earthly friends may fail us,
And change with changing years,
This Friend is always worthy
Of that dear Name He bears.

There's a crown for little children
Above the bright blue sky,
And all who look for Jesus
Shall wear it by and by;
A crown of brightest glory,
Which He will then bestow
On those who found his favor
And loved His Name below.

There's a song for little children
Above the bright blue sky,
A song that will not weary,
Though sung continually;
A song which even angels
Can never, never sing
They know not Christ as Savior,
But worship Him as King.

There's a robe for little children
Above the bright blue sky,
And a harp of sweetest music,
And psalms of victory.
All, all above is treasured,
And found in Christ alone:
O come, dear little children
That all may be your own.

About the writer: Albert Midlane, an English layman, was born in Newport, Isle of Wight in 1825. During his lifetime he wrote over 800 hymns. He attributed his interest in and contributions to hymnology to the suggestion and encouragement of a favorite Sunday school teacher. He once wrote: "Most of my hymns have been written during walks around the ancient and historic ruins of Carisbrooke Castle. The twilight hour, so dear to thought, and the hushed serenity then pervading nature have often allured my soul to deep and uninterrupted meditation, which, in its turn, has given birth to lines which, had not these walks been taken, would never probably have been penned." **Key Verse:** Then he took the children into his arms and placed his hands on their heads and blessed them. –Mark 10:16

◆ 74 ◆

THE LORD WILL COME AND NOT BE SLOW
The Lord will come and not be slow;
His footsteps cannot err;
Before Him righteousness shall go,
His royal harbinger.

Mercy and truth, that long were missed,
Now joyfully are met;
Sweet peace and righteousness have kissed,
And hand in hand are set.

Truth from the earth, like to a flower,
Shall bud and blossom then,
And justice, from her heavenly bower,
Look down on mortal men.

Thee will I praise, O Lord, my God!
Thee honor and adore
With my whole heart; and blaze abroad
Thy Name forevermore!

About the writer: John Milton, one of the greatest of English poets, is known to hymnologists as the Puritan author of 19 versions of various Psalms, which appeared in his *Poems in English and Latin*, 1673. Milton was born in London in 1608 and died in the same city in 1674. He was educated at Cambridge. In 1652 he became totally blind – a condition that did not keep him from writing such works as the epic "Paradise Lost." **Key Verse:** See, I am coming soon, and my reward is with me, to repay all according to their deeds. –Revelation 22:12

◆ **75** ◆

LORD OF THE LIVING HARVEST

Lord of the living harvest
That whitens o'er the plain,
Where angels soon shall gather
Their sheaves of golden grain,
Accept these hands to labor,
These hearts to trust and love,
And deign with them to hasten
Thy kingdom from above.

As laborers in Thy vineyard,
Lord, send them out to be
Content to bear the burden
Of weary days for Thee.
To ask no other wages
When Thou shalt call them home
But to have shared the travail
Which makes Thy kingdom come.

Be with them, God the Father;
Be with them, God the Son;
And God the Holy Spirit,
Most Blessed Three in One.
Make them Thy faithful servants
Thee rightly to adore
And fill them with Thy fullness
Both now and evermore.

About the writer: John Samuel Bewley Monsell, a clergyman in the Church of England, was born in Londonderry, Ireland in 1811. He was educated at Trinity College, Dublin. He took holy orders in 1834 and served in several offices of the Church of England. His death in 1875 was caused by his falling from the roof of his church, which was at the time under construction. He wrote a large number of hymns, some 300 in all being published in the six different volumes which he issued between 1837 and 1873. **Key Verse:** These were his instructions to them: "The harvest is so great, but the workers are so few. Pray to the Lord who is in charge of the harvest, and ask him to send out more workers for his fields. –Luke 10:2

◆ **76** ◆

O BLESS THE LORD, MY SOUL
O bless the Lord, my soul!
His grace to thee proclaim!
And all that is within me join
To bless His holy Name!

O bless the Lord, my soul!
His mercies bear in mind!
Forget not all His benefits!
The Lord to thee is kind.

He pardons all thy sins;
Prolongs thy feeble breath;
He healeth thine infirmities,
And ransoms thee from death.

Then bless His holy Name,
Whose grace hath made thee whole,
Whose lovingkindness
    crowns thy days!
O bless the Lord, my soul!

About the writer: James Montgomery, the son of a Moravian minister; was born in Ayrshire, Scotland in 1771. He became a renowned poet and abandoned the Christian faith. At the age of 43 he repented of his sinful condition and joined the Moravian congregation at Fulneck. He expressed his feelings at the time in the following lines: People of the living God / I have sought the world around, / Paths of sin and sorrow trod, / Peace and comfort nowhere found. / Now to you my spirit turns– / Turns a fugitive unblest; / Brethren, where your altar burns, / O receive me into rest. He died quietly in his sleep in 1854. **Key Verse:** Praise the LORD, I tell myself; with my whole heart, I will praise his holy name. –Psalm 103:1

◆ **77** ◆

COME, YE DISCONSOLATE
Come, ye disconsolate, where'er ye languish,
Come to the mercy seat, fervently kneel.
Here bring your wounded hearts, here tell your anguish;
Earth has no sorrow that heaven cannot heal.

Joy of the desolate, light of the straying,
Hope of the penitent, fadeless and pure!
Here speaks the Comforter, tenderly saying,
"Earth has no sorrow that heaven cannot cure."

Here see the bread of life, see waters flowing
Forth from the throne of God, pure from above.
Come to the feast of love; come, ever knowing
Earth has no sorrow but heaven can remove.

About the writer: Thomas Moore, the noted Irish poet, was born in Dublin in 1779. He graduated from Trinity College, in his native city, in 1798, and the following year moved to London and began the study of law. From 1800 until his death in 1852, he published works in prose and poetry including *Sacred Songs*, 1816. **Key Verse:** The young women will dance for joy, and the men–old and young–will join in the celebration. I will turn their mourning into joy. I will comfort them and exchange their sorrow for rejoicing. –Jeremiah 31:13

◆ 78 ◆

MY HOPE IS BUILT
My hope is built on nothing less
Than Jesus' blood and righteousness.
I dare not trust the sweetest frame,
But wholly trust in Jesus' Name.

> *Refrain*
> *On Christ the solid Rock I stand,*
> *All other ground is sinking sand;*
> *All other ground is sinking sand.*

When darkness seems to hide His face,
I rest on His unchanging grace.
In every high and stormy gale,
My anchor holds within the veil. *Refrain*

His oath, His covenant, His blood,
Support me in the whelming flood.
When all around my soul gives way,
He then is all my Hope and Stay. *Refrain*

When He shall come with trumpet sound,
Oh may I then in Him be found.
Dressed in His righteousness alone,
Faultless to stand before the throne. *Refrain*

About the writer: Edward Mote, an English Baptist minister, was born in London in 1797. He was a cabinetmaker for some years but eventually entered the ministry. From 1852 until his death in 1874 he was pastor of the Baptist Church in Essex. He wrote more than 100 hymns. **Key Verses:** Though the rain comes in torrents and the floodwaters rise and the winds beat against that house, it won't collapse, because it is built on rock. But anyone who hears my teaching and ignores it is foolish, like a person who builds a house on sand. –Matthew 7:25, 26

◆ 79 ◆

WE MARCH TO VICTORY

Refrain
We march, we march to victory,
With the cross of the Lord before us,
With His loving eye looking down from the sky,
And His holy arm spread o'er us,
His holy arm spread o'er us.

We come in the might of the Lord of light,
With armor bright to meet Him;
And we put to flight the armies of night,
That the sons of the day may greet Him,
The sons of day may greet Him. *Refrain*

Our sword is the Spirit of God on high,
Our helmet is His salvation,
Our banner the cross of Calvary.
Our watchword, the Incarnation,
Our watchword, the Incarnation. *Refrain*

Then onward we march, our arms to prove,
With the banner of Christ before us,
With His eye of love looking down from above,
And His holy arm spread o'er us,
His holy arm spread o'er us. *Refrain*

About the writer: Gerard Moultrie, a clergyman in the Church of England, was born in 1829 in Rugby, England. Among his published volumes were *Hymns and Lyrics for the Seasons and Saints' Days of the Church*, 1867. His hymns include translations from the Latin, Greek, and German. **Key Verse:** How we thank God, who gives us victory over sin and death through Jesus Christ our Lord! –1 Corinthians 15:57

• 80 •

SHOUT THE GLAD TIDINGS
> *Refrain*
> *Shout the glad tidings, exultingly sing,*
> *Jerusalem triumphs, Messiah is King!*

Zion, the marvelous story be telling,
The Son of the Highest, how lowly His birth!
The brightest archangel in glory excelling,
He stoops to redeem thee, He reigns upon earth. *Refrain*

Tell how He cometh; from nation to nation
The heart cheering news let the earth echo round;
How free to the faithful He offers salvation,
His people with joy everlasting are crowned. *Refrain*

Mortals, your homage be gratefully bringing,
And sweet let the gladsome hosannas arise;
Ye angels, the full alleluias be singing;
One chorus resound through the earth and the skies. *Refrain*

About the writer: William Augustus Muhlenberg, an Episcopal minister, was born in Philadelphia in 1796. He graduated from the University of Pennsylvania in 1814 and was ordained priest in the Episcopal Church in 1820. Subsequently he established St. Paul's College at Flushing, Long Island. From 1846 to 1859 he was rector of the Church of the Holy Communion in New York City. In 1855 he founded St. Luke's Hospital in New York City, and was its pastor and superintendent until his death. Dr. Muhlenberg was one of the committee that edited *Hymns Suited to the Feasts and Fasts of the Church*, 1826. He died in 1871. **Key Verse:** (B)ut the angel reassured them. "Don't be afraid!" he said. "I bring you good news of great joy for everyone!" –Luke 2:10

• 81 •

AROUND THE THRONE OF GOD A BAND
Around the throne of God a band
Of bright and glorious angels stand;

Sweet harps within their hands they hold,
And on their heads are crowns of gold.

Some wait around Him ready still
To sing His praise and do His will,
And some, when He commands them, go
To guard His servants here below.

Lord, give Thine angels every day
Command to guard us on our way,
And bid them every evening keep
Their watch around us while we sleep.

So shall no wicked thing draw near
To do us harm or cause us fear;
And we shall dwell, when life is past,
With angels round Thy throne at last.

About the writer: John Mason Neale, an English clergyman and author, was born in London in 1818. He graduated from Cambridge in 1840 and the following year entered the ministry. He was appointed warden of Sackville College, Sussex, an institution for aged women, in 1846; an office he continued to fill until his death in 1866. He was the author of numerous published works including 15 volumes of hymns and translations. **Key Verse:** For he orders his angels to protect you wherever you go. –Psalm 91:11

❖ 82 ❖

LEAD, KINDLY LIGHT
Lead, kindly Light, amid th'encircling gloom, lead Thou me on!
The night is dark, and I am far from home; lead Thou me on!
Keep Thou my feet; I do not ask to see
The distant scene; one step enough for me.

I was not ever thus, nor prayed that Thou shouldst lead me on;
I loved to choose and see my path; but now lead Thou me on!

I loved the garish day, and, spite of fears,
Pride ruled my will. Remember not past years!

So long Thy power hath blest me, sure it still will lead me on.
O'er moor and fen, o'er crag and torrent, till the night is gone,
And with the morn those angel faces smile, which I
Have loved long since, and lost awhile!

Meantime, along the narrow rugged path, Thyself hast trod,
Lead, Savior, lead me home in childlike faith, home to my God.
To rest forever after earthly strife
In the calm light of everlasting life.

About the writer: John Henry Newman, a cardinal in the Roman Catholic Church, was born in London in 1801. He graduated from Oxford in 1820 and for several years was a tutor at that college. He was a leader of the High Church party in the Church of England and had great influence among the young men at Oxford. He was ordained to the ministry in the Church of England in 1824 but in 1845 joined the Catholic Church. He died in London in 1890. He was the most prominent and influential English Roman Catholic of the nineteenth century. His collected works include many volumes on doctrinal and ecclesiastical subjects. His translations of Latin hymns and his original hymns are found in *Verses on Various Occasions*, 1868. **Key Verse:** Your word is a lamp for my feet and a light for my path. –Psalm 119:105

◆ 83 ◆

AMAZING GRACE
Amazing grace! How sweet the sound
That saved a wretch like me!
I once was lost, but now am found;
Was blind, but now I see.

'Twas grace that taught my heart to fear,
And grace my fears relieved;
How precious did that grace appear
The hour I first believed.

Through many dangers, toils and snares,
I have already come;
'Tis grace hath brought me safe thus far,
And grace will lead me home.

The Lord has promised good to me,
His Word my hope secures;
He will my Shield and Portion be,
As long as life endures.

Yea, when this flesh and heart shall fail,
And mortal life shall cease,
I shall possess, within the veil,
A life of joy and peace.

The earth shall soon dissolve like snow,
The sun forbear to shine;
But God, Who called me here below,
Shall be forever mine.

When we've been there ten thousand years,
Bright shining as the sun,
We've no less days to sing God's praise
Than when we'd first begun.

About the writer: John Newton was born in London in 1725. His mother, a pious woman, died when he was only seven years of age. His only "schooling" was from his eighth to his tenth year. He was engaged in the African slave trade for several years, and was even himself held as a slave at one time in Sierra Leone. He bragged of his sinful nature, but was converted in a storm at sea while returning from Africa. He married a devout Christian in 1750 and became a minister in the Established Church in 1758, preaching at a church in Olney, near Cambridge. He remained here for nearly sixteen years, becoming friends with the poet William Cowper, who was joint author with him of the *Olney Hymns*, 1779. Soon after the appearance of this volume he moved to London where he was rector of St. Mary Woolnoth. He

died in 1807. Newton wrote his own epitaph, which included the following:
John Newton, once an infidel and libertine, was, by the rich mercy of our
Lord and Saviour Jesus Christ, preserved, restored, and pardoned, and
appointed to preach the Faith he had long labored to destroy. **Key Verse:** "I
don't know whether he is a sinner," the man replied. "But I know this: I was
blind, and now I can see!" –John 9:25

◆ 84 ◆

WHERE CROSS THE CROWDED WAYS OF LIFE
Where cross the crowded ways of life,
Where sound the cries of race and clan
Above the noise of selfish strife,
We hear your voice, O Son of man.

In haunts of wretchedness and need,
On shadowed thresholds dark with fears,
From paths where hide the lures of greed,
We catch the vision of Your tears.

The cup of water given for You,
Still holds the freshness of Your grace;
Yet long these multitudes to view
The sweet compassion of Your face.

Till sons of men shall learn Your love
And follow where Your feet have trod,
Till, glorious from Your heaven above,
Shall come the city of our God!

About the writer: Frank Mason North, a minister in the Methodist Episcopal
Church, was born in New York in 1850. He graduated from Wesleyan
University in 1872 and entered the ministry that same year. After serving in
various posts for twenty years, he became, in 1892, corresponding secretary
of the New York City Church Extension and Missionary Society, a role he
filled until his death. He contributed various hymns to the periodical *Christian*

City. **Key Verse:** Now go out to the street corners and invite everyone you see. –Matthew 22:9

♦ **85** ♦

O THOU GOD OF MY SALVATION
O Thou God of my salvation, my Redeemer from all sin;
Moved by Thy divine compassion, Who hast died my heart to win;
I will praise Thee, I will praise Thee, where shall I Thy praise begin?
I will praise Thee, I will praise Thee, where shall I Thy praise begin?

Though unseen, I love the Savior, He hath brought salvation near;
Manifests His pardoning favor, and when Jesus doth appear,
Soul and body, soul and body, shall His glorious image bear;
Soul and body, soul and body, shall His glorious image bear.

While the angel choirs are crying, "Glory to the great I Am,"
I with them will still be vying—glory, glory, to the Lamb!
Oh, how precious, oh, how precious is the sound of Jesus' Name!
Oh, how precious, oh, how precious is the sound of Jesus' Name!

Angels now are hovering round us, unperceived among the throng;
Wondering at the love that crowned us, glad to sing the holy song;
Hallelujah, hallelujah, love and praise to Christ belong!
Hallelujah, hallelujah, love and praise to Christ belong!

About the writer: Thomas Olivers was born in Tregoman, Wales in 1725. Early in life he was left an orphan. Distant relatives brought him up in an indifferent manner. He was sent to school for a time, and later became an apprentice to a shoemaker; a man who treated him so cruelly that he ran away. He turned to alcohol for comfort until he heard George Whitefield preach and he was converted. He later wrote, "When the sermon began I was one of the most abandoned and profligate young men living; before it was ended I was a new creature." From that time onward he lived a new life. In 1753 he became one of John Wesley's itinerant preachers, working tirelessly for 46 years. He wrote only four or five hymns, but each was deemed by Wesley to be among the best he had seen – a high compliment. He died in

1799. **Key Verse:** Lead me by your truth and teach me, for you are the God who saves me. All day long I put my hope in you. –Psalm 25:5

◆ 86 ◆

MY FAITH LOOKS UP TO THEE
My faith looks up to Thee,
Thou Lamb of Calvary, Savior divine!
Now hear me while I pray, take all my guilt away,
O let me from this day be wholly Thine!

May Thy rich grace impart
Strength to my fainting heart, my zeal inspire!
As Thou hast died for me, O may my love to Thee,
Pure warm, and changeless be, a living fire!

While life's dark maze I tread,
And griefs around me spread, be Thou my Guide;
Bid darkness turn to day, wipe sorrow's tears away,
Nor let me ever stray from Thee aside.

When ends life's transient dream,
When death's cold sullen stream over me roll;
Blest Savior, then in love, fear and distrust remove;
O bear me safe above, a ransomed soul!

About the writer: Ray Palmer, a Congregational minister, was born in Little Compton, Rhode Island in 1808. At 13 he became a clerk in a dry goods store in Boston where he joined the Park Street Congregational Church. That church's pastor, Dr. S.E. Dwight, discerned his promise and took a deep interest in him – helping him get into Phillips Academy, Andover and later Yale College. After graduating in 1820 he moved to New York City, taking up the study of theology privately and supporting himself by teaching in a woman's college. He taught in a young ladies' institute at New Haven during 1832-1834, continuing his theological studies and entering the ministry at the close of this period. From 1835 to 1850 he was pastor of the Congregational Church in Bath, Maine and from 1850 to 1865 he was pastor of the First

Congregational Church of Albany, New York. He served other posts but finally retired in 1878. He moved to Newark, New Jersey where he died in 1887. Between 1829 and 1881 he published eleven volumes, among them *Hymns and Sacred Pieces*, 1865. *Julian's Dictionary of Hymnology* states that "the best of his hymns, by their combination of thought, poetry, and devotion, are superior to almost all others of American origin." **Key Verse:** That is why we live by believing and not by seeing. –2 Corinthians 5:7

◆ 87 ◆
ALL HAIL THE POWER OF JESUS' NAME
All hail the power of Jesus' Name! Let angels prostrate fall;
Bring forth the royal diadem, and crown Him Lord of all.
Bring forth the royal diadem, and crown Him Lord of all.

Let highborn seraphs tune the lyre, and as they tune it, fall
Before His face Who tunes their choir, and crown Him Lord of all.
Before His face Who tunes their choir, and crown Him Lord of all.

Crown Him, ye morning stars of light, Who fixed this floating ball;
Now hail the strength of Israel's might, and crown Him Lord of all.
Now hail the strength of Israel's might, and crown Him Lord of all.

Crown Him, ye martyrs of your God, who from His altar call;
Extol the Stem of Jesse's Rod, and crown Him Lord of all.
Extol the Stem of Jesse's Rod, and crown Him Lord of all.

Hail Him, ye heirs of David's line, Whom David Lord did call,
The God incarnate, Man divine, and crown Him Lord of all,
The God incarnate, Man divine, and crown Him Lord of all.

Sinners, whose love can ne'er forget the wormwood and the gall,
Go spread your trophies at His feet, and crown Him Lord of all.
Go spread your trophies at His feet, and crown Him Lord of all.

Let every tribe and every tongue before Him prostrate fall
And shout in universal song the crownèd Lord of all.
And shout in universal song the crownèd Lord of all.

About the writer: Edward Perronet, an Independent English clergyman,
was born in 1726. He was the son of Vincent Perronet, vicar of Shoreham,
who was a friend and supporter of the Wesleys. Edward was educated in the
Church of England but became a Wesleyan preacher. In 1756 the question
arose among the Methodists concerning separation from the Church of
England. The Wesleys strenuously opposed this move; Perronet as strongly
favored and urged it. He later joined the Independent or Dissenting Church,
where he remained until his death in 1792. **Key Verses:** Because of this, God
raised him up to the heights of heaven and gave him a name that is above
every other name, so that at the name of Jesus every knee will bow, in heaven
and on earth and under the earth, and every tongue will confess that Jesus
Christ is Lord, to the glory of God the Father. –Philippians 2:9-11

◆ 88 ◆

FOR THE BEAUTY OF THE EARTH
For the beauty of the earth
For the glory of the skies,
For the love which from our birth
Over and around us lies.

> *Refrain*
> *Lord of all, to Thee we raise,*
> *This our hymn of grateful praise.*

For the beauty of each hour,
Of the day and of the night,
Hill and vale, and tree and flower,
Sun and moon, and stars of light. *Refrain*

For the joy of ear and eye,
For the heart and mind's delight,
For the mystic harmony
Linking sense to sound and sight. *Refrain*

For the joy of human love,
Brother, sister, parent, child,
Friends on earth and friends above,
For all gentle thoughts and mild. *Refrain*

For Thy Church, that evermore
Lifteth holy hands above,
Offering upon every shore
Her pure sacrifice of love. *Refrain*

For each perfect gift of Thine,
To our race so freely given,
Graces human and divine,
Flowers of earth and buds of Heaven. *Refrain*

About the writer: Folliott Sanford Pierpoint was born in Bath, England in 1835. He was educated at Queen's College, Cambridge, graduating in 1871. He published a volume of poems in 1878 and contributed a few hymns to the *Churchman's Companion*, *Lyra Eucharistica*, and other publications. He was a life-long member of the Church of England. **Key Verse:** In a great chorus they sang, "Holy, holy, holy is the LORD Almighty! The whole earth is filled with his glory!" –Isaiah 6:3

◆ 89 ◆

I DO NOT ASK, O LORD
I do not ask, O Lord, that life may be
A pleasant road;
I do not ask that Thou wouldst take from me
Aught of its load.

I do not ask that flowers should always spring
Beneath my feet;
I know too well the poison and the sting
Of things too sweet.

For one thing, only Lord, dear Lord, I plead:
Lead me aright,
Though strength should falter and though heart should bleed,
Through peace to light.

Joy is like restless day; but peace divine
Like quiet night:
Lead me, O Lord, till perfect day shall shine,
Through peace to light.

About the writer: Adelaide Anne Proctor was born in London in 1825 and died there in 1864. Her hymns were published in her book *Legends and Lyrics*, 1858. In 1851 she became a member of the Roman Catholic Church. She was highly regarded for her skills as a linguist. **Key Verse:** You are my rock and my fortress. For the honor of your name, lead me out of this peril. –Psalm 31:3

◆ 90 ◆

JESUS, MEEK AND GENTLE

Jesus, meek and gentle,
Son of God most high,
Gracious, loving Savior,
Hear Thy children's cry.

Pardon our offenses,
Loose our captive chains,
Break down every idol
Which our soul detains.

Give us holy freedom,
Fill our hearts with love;
Draw us, holy Jesus,
To the realms above.

Jesus, meek and gentle,
Son of God most high,
Gracious, loving Savior,
Hear Thy children's cry.
Hear Thy children's cry.

About the writer: George Rundle Prynne, an English clergyman of the Established Church, was born in Cornwall, England in 1818. He was educated at Cambridge and was ordained to the ministry in 1841. He became vicar of St. Peter's, in Plymouth, in 1848. Among his publications were three volumes of sermons and *Hymnal Suited for the Services of the Church*, 1858. He died in 1903. **Key Verse:** Take my yoke upon you. Let me teach you, because I am humble and gentle, and you will find rest for your souls. –Matthew 11:29

• 91 •

GOD BE WITH YOU TILL WE MEET AGAIN
God be with you till we meet again;
By His counsels guide, uphold you,
With His sheep securely fold you;
God be with you till we meet again.

> *Refrain*
> *Till we meet, till we meet,*
> *Till we meet at Jesus' feet;*
> *Till we meet, till we meet,*
> *God be with you till we meet again.*

God be with you till we meet again;
Neath His wings protecting hide you;
Daily manna still provide you;
God be with you till we meet again. *Refrain*

God be with you till we meet again;
When life's perils thick confound you;
Put His arms unfailing round you;
God be with you till we meet again. *Refrain*

God be with you till we meet again;
Of His promises remind you;
For life's upper garner bind you;
God be with you till we meet again. *Refrain*

God be with you till we meet again;
Ended when for you earth's story,
Israel's chariot sweep to glory;
God be with you till we meet again. *Refrain*

About the writer: Jeremiah Eames Rankin, a Congregational minister and educator, was born in Thornton, New Hampshire in 1828. After graduating from Middlebury College in 1848 he became a pastor at various New England Congregational Churches. From 1889 to 1903 he was President of Howard University. He was also the author of about a dozen volumes of prose and poetry and , in 1878, he edited and issued the *Gospel Temperance Hymnal*. He died in 1904. **Key Verse:** Teach these new disciples to obey all the commands I have given you. And be sure of this: I am with you always, even to the end of the age. –Matthew 28:20

◆ **92** ◆

SPIRIT DIVINE, ATTEND OUR PRAYER
Spirit divine, attend our prayer,
And make our heart Thy home;
Descend with all Thy gracious power;
Come, Holy Spirit, come.

Come as the light! to us reveal
The truth we long to know;
Reveal the narrow path of right,
The way of duty show.

Come as the dew, and sweetly bless
This consecrated hour;
May barrenness rejoice to own
Thy fertilizing power.

Come as the dove, and spread Thy wings,
The wings of peaceful love;
And let Thy Church on earth become
Blest as Thy Church above.

Spirit divine, attend our prayer;
Make a lost world Thy home;
Descend with all thy gracious powers,
O come, great Spirit, come.

About the writer: Andrew Reed, an English Independent minister, was born in London in 1787. He graduated from Hackney College and soon afterwards became pastor of a Church in East London where he remained for fifty years. He died in London in 1862. He is best known in England as the founder of the London Orphan Asylum. He wrote nearly 30 hymns. **Key Verse:** Suddenly, there was a sound from heaven like the roaring of a mighty windstorm in the skies above them, and it filled the house where they were meeting. –Acts 2:2

◆ **93** ◆

MY SOUL BEFORE THEE PROSTRATE LIES
My soul before Thee prostrate lies;
To Thee, her Source, my spirit flies;
My wants I mourn, my chains I see;
O let Thy presence set me free.

Jesus, vouchsafe my heart and will
With Thy meek lowliness to fill;
No more her power let nature boast,
But in Thy will may mine be lost.

Already springing hope I feel,
God will destroy the power of hell,
And, from a land of wars and pain,
Lead me where peace and safety reign.

One only care my soul shall know,
Father, all Thy commands to do;
And feel, what endless years shall prove,
That Thou, my Lord, my God, art love.

About the writer: Christian Frederic Richter was born in Silesia in 1676. He graduated from the University of Halle and worked at the orphanage there. He was a student of medicine as well as of theology. He wrote about 30 hymns before his death in 1711. **Key Verse:** Let me hear you say, "I am your salvation!" –Psalm 35:3b

◆ 94 ◆

COME, THOU FOUNT OF EVERY BLESSING

Come, Thou Fount of every blessing,
Tune my heart to sing Thy grace;
Streams of mercy, never ceasing,
Call for songs of loudest praise.
Teach me some melodious sonnet,
Sung by flaming tongues above.
Praise the mount! I'm fixed upon it,
Mount of Thy redeeming love.

O to grace how great a debtor
Daily I'm constrained to be!
Let Thy goodness, like a fetter,
Bind my wandering heart to Thee.
Prone to wander, Lord, I feel it,
Prone to leave the God I love;
Here's my heart, O take and seal it,
Seal it for Thy courts above.

O that day when freed from sinning,
I shall see Thy lovely face;
Clothed then in blood washed linen
How I'll sing Thy sovereign grace;
Come, my Lord, no longer tarry,
Take my ransomed soul away;
Send thine angels now to carry
Me to realms of endless day.

About the writer: Robert Robinson, a Baptist minister, was born in Norfolk, England in 1735. At the age of 14 he was apprenticed to a London hairdresser. He was converted among the Methodists at the age of 20 and became a lay preacher. In less than a year, however, he became pastor of the Baptist Church at Cambridge. He died in 1790. He was a very popular preacher and wrote a number of well-known hymns. **Key Verse:** Samuel then took a large stone and placed it between the towns of Mizpah and Jeshanah. He named it Ebenezer–"the stone of help"–for he said, "Up to this point the LORD has helped us!" –1 Samuel 7:12

◆ 95 ◆

WHAT A FRIEND WE HAVE IN JESUS

What a Friend we have in Jesus, all our sins and griefs to bear!
What a privilege to carry everything to God in prayer!
O what peace we often forfeit, O what needless pain we bear,
All because we do not carry everything to God in prayer.

Have we trials and temptations? Is there trouble anywhere?
We should never be discouraged; take it to the Lord in prayer.
Can we find a friend so faithful who will all our sorrows share?
Jesus knows our every weakness; take it to the Lord in prayer.

Are we weak and heavy laden, cumbered with a load of care?
Precious Savior, still our refuge, take it to the Lord in prayer.
Do your friends despise, forsake you? Take it to the Lord in prayer!
In His arms He'll take and shield you; you will find a solace there.

Blessed Savior, Thou hast promised Thou wilt all our burdens bear
May we ever, Lord, be bringing all to Thee in earnest prayer.
Soon in glory bright unclouded there will be no need for prayer
Rapture, praise and endless worship will be our sweet portion there.

About the writer: Joseph Scriven was born in Dublin in 1820 and graduated from Trinity College, Dublin. He moved to Canada in 1845 where he led a humble life until his death in 1886. Ira D. Sankey, in his *Story of the Gospel Hymns*, wrote that "the young lady to whom Scriven was to be married was accidentally drowned on the eve of their wedding day. This sad event led him to consecrate his life and property to the service of Christ. It is said that no service was too lowly for him to render if it could be done without compensation and without observation for one of the least of Christ's disciples." **Key Verse:** And here is how to measure it–the greatest love is shown when people lay down their lives for their friends. –John 15:13

♦ 96 ♦

RISE, MY SOUL, AND STRETCH THY WINGS

Rise, my soul, and stretch thy wings, thy better portion trace;
Rise from transitory things, towards heaven, thy destined place:
Sun and moon and stars decay, time shall soon this earth remove;
Rise, my soul, and haste away to seats prepared above.

Rivers to the ocean run, nor stay in all their course;
Fire ascending seeks the sun; both speed them to their source:
So my soul, derived from God, longs to view His glorious face,
Forward tends to His abode, to rest in His embrace.

Cease, ye pilgrims, cease to mourn, press onward to the prize;
Soon thy Savior will return, to take thee to the skies:
There is everlasting peace, rest, enduring rest, in heaven;
There will sorrow ever cease, and crowns of joy be given.

About the writer: Robert Seagrave was an English clergyman who was born in 1693 and graduated from Cambridge in 1718. He defended the Calvinistic Methodists and wrote and published pamphlets and sermons designed to reform the clergy and Church of England. While preaching at Lorimer's Hall, London, he published a hymn book for the use of his congregation: *Hymns for Christian Worship*, 1742. To this book he contributed 50 original hymns. The year of his death is not known. **Key Verse:** There are many rooms in my Father's home, and I am going to prepare a place for you. If this were not so, I would tell you plainly. –John 14:2

♦ 97 ♦

MY COUNTRY 'TIS OF THEE

My country, 'tis of thee,
Sweet land of liberty,
Of thee I sing;
Land where my fathers died,
Land of the pilgrims' pride,
From every mountainside,
Let freedom ring!

My native country, thee,
Land of the noble free,
Thy name I love;
I love thy rocks and rills,
Thy woods and templed hills;
My heart with rapture thrills,
Like that above.

Let music swell the breeze,
And ring from all the trees,
Sweet freedom's song;
Let mortal tongues awake;
Let all that breathe partake;
Let rocks their silence break,
The sound prolong.

Our fathers' God, to Thee,
Author of liberty,
To Thee we sing;
Long may our land be bright
With freedom's holy light;
Protect us by Thy might,
Great God, our King.

About the writer: Samuel Francis Smith, a Baptist minister, was born in Boston in 1808. He attended the Boston Latin School and entered Harvard College in 1825. After leaving Harvard in 1829 he entered Andover Theological Seminary, graduating in 1832. His first pastorate was at Waterville, Maine where he remained eight years. In 1842 he became the pastor of the First Baptist Church in Newton, Massachusetts. He resigned this position in 1854 and became the editor of the *Baptist Missionary Union*. He helped prepare the Baptist collection of hymns titled *The Psalmist*, 1843. He died in 1895. **Key Verse:** And you will know the truth, and the truth will set you free. –John 8:32

◆ **98** ◆

IT IS WELL WITH MY SOUL
When peace, like a river, attendeth my way,
When sorrows like sea billows roll;
Whatever my lot, Thou has taught me to say,
It is well, it is well, with my soul.

> *Refrain*
> *It is well, with my soul,*
> *It is well, with my soul,*
> *It is well, it is well, with my soul.*

Though Satan should buffet, though trials should come,
Let this blest assurance control,
That Christ has regarded my helpless estate,
And hath shed His own blood for my soul. *Refrain*

My sin, oh, the bliss of this glorious thought!
My sin, not in part but the whole,
Is nailed to the cross, and I bear it no more,
Praise the Lord, praise the Lord, O my soul! *Refrain*

For me, be it Christ, be it Christ hence to live:
If Jordan above me shall roll,
No pang shall be mine, for in death as in life
Thou wilt whisper Thy peace to my soul. *Refrain*

But, Lord, 'tis for Thee, for Thy coming we wait,
The sky, not the grave, is our goal;
Oh trump of the angel! Oh voice of the Lord!
Blessed hope, Blessed rest of my soul! *Refrain*

And Lord, haste the day when my faith shall be sight,
The clouds be rolled back as a scroll;
The trump shall resound, and the Lord shall descend,
Even so, it is well with my soul. *Refrain*

About the writer: Horatio G. Spafford was a wealthy Chicago businessman who lost his fortune during the Chicago fire. Despite this, he and his wife, Anna, devoted countless hours to helping the survivors. Later he sent Anna and his four daughters to England for a rest. While crossing the Atlantic their ship sank in a collision. Anna survived and sent him the heartbreaking telegram, "Saved Alone." Several weeks later, as Spafford's own ship passed near the spot where his daughters died, he wrote the hymn "It Is Well With My Soul." In 1881 the Spaffords moved to Jerusalem – taking two daughters born after the ship-wreck – and helped found a group called the American Colony; its mission was to serve the poor. The colony later became the subject of the Nobel prize winning *Jerusalem*, by Swedish novelist Selma Lagerlöf. Few hymn stories are as powerful as this one. **Key Verse:** Praise the LORD! Praise the LORD, I tell myself. –Psalm 146:1

◆ 99 ◆

O HAPPY HOME
O happy home, where Thou art loved the dearest,
Thou loving Friend and Savior of our race,
And where among the guests there never cometh
One who can hold such high and honored place!

O happy home, where two in heart united
In holy faith and Blessed hope are one,
Whom death a little while alone divideth,
And cannot end the union here begun!

O happy home, whose little ones are given
Early to Thee, in humble faith and prayer,
To Thee, their Friend, Who from the heights of Heaven
Guides them, and guards with more than mother's care!

Until at last, when earth's day's work is ended,
All meet Thee in the Blessed home above,
From whence Thou camest, where Thou hast ascended,
Thy everlasting home of peace and love!

About the writer: Karl Johann Philipp Spitta, a German theologian and poet, was born in Hanover in 1801. He was apprenticed to a watchmaker as a young man. While learning this trade he began the study of languages and, in 1821, entered the University of Gottingen to study theology. After graduating he was engaged as tutor to a wealthy family for some time. From 1828 until his death he was the popular and successful pastor of several Lutheran Churches. He died in 1859. His *Psalter and Harfe, Leipzig*, 1833, was translated by Richard Massie in 1860. **Key Verse:** Then he brought them into his house and set a meal before them. He and his entire household rejoiced because they all believed in God. –Acts 16:34

◆ 100 ◆

HE IS GONE, A CLOUD OF LIGHT
He is gone—a cloud of light
Has received Him from our sight;
High in Heav'n, where eye of men
Follows not, nor angels' ken;
Through the veils of time and space,
Passed into the holiest place;
All the toil, the sorrow done,
All the battle fought and won.

He is gone—and we remain
In this world of sin and pain:
In the void which He has left
On this earth, of Him bereft.
We have still His work to do,
We can still His path pursue;
Seek Him both in friend and foe,
In ourselves His image show.

He is gone—but we once more
Shall behold Him as before;
In the heaven of heavens the same,
As on earth He went and came;
In the many mansions there,
Place for us He will prepare;
In that world unseen, unknown,
He and we shall yet be one.

He is gone—but not in vain,
Wait until He comes again:
He is risen, He is not here,
Far above this earthly sphere;
Evermore in heart and mind

There our peace in Him we find:
To our own eternal Friend,
Thitherward let us ascend.

About the writer: Arthur Penrhyn Stanley was born in Cheshire, England in
1815. He graduated from Oxford in 1837 and entered the ministry of the
Church of England. In 1855 he was appointed Regius Professor of
Ecclesiastical History at Oxford. In 1864 he became Dean of Westminster.
That same year he married Lady Augusta Bruce, a personal friend and
attendant of Queen Victoria. He was the author of about a dozen hymns and
of several translations. He was also a noted historian and biographer. He died
in 1881. **Key Verse:** It was not long after he said this that he was taken up
into the sky while they were watching, and he disappeared into a cloud.
–Acts 1:9

♦ **101** ♦

ON JORDAN'S STORMY BANKS I STAND
On Jordan's stormy banks I stand,
And cast a wishful eye
To Canaan's fair and happy land,
Where my possessions lie.

> *Refrain*
> *I am bound for the promised land,*
> *I am bound for the promised land;*
> *Oh who will come and go with me?*
> *I am bound for the promised land.*

O the transporting, rapturous scene,
That rises to my sight!
Sweet fields arrayed in living green,
And rivers of delight! *Refrain*

When I shall reach that happy place,
I'll be forever blest,
For I shall see my Father's face,
And in His bosom rest. *Refrain*

Filled with delight my raptured soul
Would here no longer stay;
Though Jordan's waves around me roll,
Fearless I'd launch away. *Refrain*

About the writer: Samuel Stennett, an English Baptist minister, was born in Exeter in 1727. In 1758 he succeeded his father as pastor of the Wild Street Church in London where he remained for 37 years. He died in 1795. Stennett was the author of some prose writings and of 38 hymns. **Key Verse:** And the city has no need of sun or moon, for the glory of God illuminates the city, and the Lamb is its light. –Revelation 21:23

✦ 102 ✦

THE CHURCH'S ONE FOUNDATION

The Church's one foundation
Is Jesus Christ her Lord,
She is His new creation
By water and the Word.
From heaven He came and sought her
To be His holy bride;
With His own blood He bought her
And for her life He died.

The Church shall never perish!
Her dear Lord to defend,
To guide, sustain, and cherish,
Is with her to the end:
Though there be those who hate her,
And false sons in her pale,
Against or foe or traitor
She ever shall prevail.

She is from every nation,
Yet one o'er all the earth;
Her charter of salvation,
One Lord, one faith, one birth;
One holy Name she blesses,
Partakes one holy food,
And to one hope she presses,
With every grace endued.

Yet she on earth hath union
With God the Three in One,
And mystic sweet communion
With those whose rest is won,
With all her sons and daughters
Who, by the Master's hand
Led through the deathly waters,
Repose in Eden land.

O happy ones and holy!
Lord, give us grace that we
Like them, the meek and lowly,
On high may dwell with Thee:
There, past the border mountains,
Where in sweet vales the Bride
With Thee by living fountains
Forever shall abide!

About the writer: Samuel John Stone, a clergyman in the Church of England, was born in Staffordshire, England in 1839. He was educated at Pembroke College, Oxford, where he graduated in 1862. He served various Churches until he succeeded his father at St. Paul's, Haggerstown in 1874. He was the author of many original hymns and translations, which were collected and published in 1886. He died in 1900. **Key Verse:** For no one can lay any other foundation than the one we already have–Jesus Christ. –1 Corinthians 3:11

✦ 103 ✦

STILL, STILL WITH THEE
Still, still with Thee, when purple morning breaketh,
When the bird waketh, and the shadows flee;
Fairer than morning, lovelier than daylight,
Dawns the sweet consciousness, I am with Thee.

Alone with Thee, amid the mystic shadows,
The solemn hush of nature newly born;
Alone with Thee in breathless adoration,
In the calm dew and freshness of the morn.

When sinks the soul, subdued by toil, to slumber,
Its closing eye looks up to Thee in prayer;
Sweet the repose beneath the wings o'ershading,
But sweeter still to wake and find Thee there.

So shall it be at last, in that bright morning,
When the soul waketh and life's shadows flee;

O in that hour, fairer than daylight dawning,
Shall rise the glorious thought, I am with Thee.

About the writer: Harriet Beecher Stowe, the daughter of the famous preacher Lyman Beecher, was born in Litchfield, Connecticut in 1812. Her father became President of Lane Theological Seminary, Cincinnati, Ohio, in 1832; and in 1833 she was married to Calvin E. Stowe, a professor in the seminary. Her book *Uncle Tom's Cabin*, which was first published in 1852 as a serial in the *National Era* magazine and later in book form, is one of the most widely known and historic volumes in the entire range of American literature. It is a work of fiction which, by means of the pathetic picture which it draws of the ills of slave life and the cruelties involved in slave ownership, did much to precipitate the American Civil War (1861-1865). Mrs. Stowe published more than forty volumes in all, many of them being works of fiction. Her *Religious Poems* appeared in 1867. She died in 1896.
Key Verse: I can't even count them; they outnumber the grains of sand! And when I wake up in the morning, you are still with me! –Psalm 139:18

◆ 104 ◆
LORD OF ALL POWER AND MIGHT

Lord of all power and might,
Father of love and light,
Speed on Thy Word!
O let the Gospel sound
All the wide world around,
Wherever man is found!
God speed His Word!

Hail, Blessed Jubilee!
Thine, Lord, the glory be;
Alleluia!
Thine was the mighty plan;
From Thee the work began;
Away with praise of man!
Glory to God!

Lo, what embattled foes,
Stern in their hate, oppose
God's holy Word!
One for His truth we stand,
Strong in His own right hand,
Firm as a martyr band:
God shield His Word!

Onward shall be our course,
Despite all fraud and force;
God is before.
His words ere long shall run
Free as the noonday sun;
His purpose must be done:
God bless His Word!

About the writer: Hugh Stowell, a minister in the Church of England, was born in 1799. He graduated from Oxford in 1822, and took holy orders the following year. He held various offices in his Church and published several ecclesial volumes. He also edited a book of hymns: *A Selection of Psalms and Hymns Suited to the Services of the Church of England*, 1831. He died in 1865. **Key Verse:** Riches and honor come from you alone, for you rule over everything. Power and might are in your hand, and it is at your discretion that people are made great and given strength. –1 Chronicles 29:12

◆ **105** ◆

'TIS MIDNIGHT, AND ON OLIVE'S BROW

'Tis midnight, and on Olive's brow
The star is dimmed that lately shone;
'Tis midnight, in the garden now
The suffering Savior prays alone.

'Tis midnight, and from all removed
Emmanuel wrestles lone with fears
E'en the disciple whom He loved
Heeds not his Master's grief and tears.

'Tis midnight, and for others' guilt
The Man of Sorrows weeps in blood;
Yet He Who hath in anguish knelt
Is not forsaken by His God.

'Tis midnight, and from ether plains
Is borne the song that angels know;
Unheard by mortals are the strains
That sweetly soothe the Savior's woe.

About the writer: William Brigham Tappan, an influential leader in Sunday school work in the Congregational Church, was born in Beverly, Massachusetts in 1794. As a young man he taught school in Philadelphia. From 1826 until his death he worked for the American Sunday School Union as a manager and superintendent. In 1841 he obtained a license to preach as a Congregational minister but was never ordained. From 1819 to 1849 he wrote and published poetry, amounting in all to eight volumes. He died in 1849. **Key Verse:** On the first day of the Festival of Unleavened Bread (the day the Passover lambs were sacrificed), Jesus' disciples asked him, "Where do you want us to go to prepare the Passover supper?" –Mark 14:12

◆ 106 ◆

AS PANTS THE HART FOR COOLING STREAMS

As pants the hart for cooling streams,
When heated in the chase,
So longs my soul, O God, for Thee
And Thy refreshing grace.

For Thee, my God, the living God,
My thirsty soul doth pine;
O, when shall I behold Thy face,
Thou majesty divine?

Why restless, why cast down, my soul?
Hope still; and thou shalt sing
The praise of Him Who is thy God,
Thy health's eternal spring.

To Father, Son, and Holy Ghost,
The God Whom we adore,
Be glory as it was, is now,
And shall be evermore.

About the writer: Nahum Tate, the English poet, was the son of an Irish clergyman and was born in Dublin in 1652. After his graduation from the University of Dublin he settled in London and entered upon a literary career. He soon won reputation as a poet and, in 1692, he became Poet Laureate. In 1696 he published the *Psalms of David Fitted to the Tunes Used in the Church*, a work that became a standard in the Anglican church for centuries. He died in 1715. **Key Verse:** As the deer pants for streams of water, so I long for you, O God. –Psalm 42:1

• **107** •

THOU HIDDEN LOVE OF GOD
Thou hidden Love of God, whose height,
Whose depth unfathomed no one knows,
I see from afar Thy beauteous light,
And only sigh for Thy repose;
My heart is pained, nor can it be
At rest, till it finds rest in Thee.

Thy secret voice invites me still
The sweetness of Thy yoke to prove;
And fain I would; but though my will
Seems fixed, yet wide my passions rove;
Yet hindrances strew all the way;
I aim at Thee, yet from Thee stray.

O hide this self from me, that I
No more, but Christ in me, may live!
My vile affections crucify,
Nor let one darling lust survive
In all things nothing may I see,
Nothing desire or seek, but Thee!

O Love, Thy sovereign aid impart
To save me from low thought care;
Chase this self will from all my heart,
From all its hidden mazes there;
Make me Thy duteous child that I
Ceaseless may "Abba, Father" cry.

Each moment draw from earth away
My heart that lowly waits Thy call;
Speak to my inmost soul and say,
"I am thy love, thy God, thy all!"
To feel Thy power, to hear Thy voice,
To taste Thy love, be all my choice.

About the writer: Gerhard Tersteegen, a pious mystic of the eighteenth century, was born in Mörs, Germany in 1697. He was apprenticed as a young man to his older brother, a shopkeeper. He purchased a humble cottage near Mühlheim, where he led a life of seclusion and self-denial for many years. At about thirty years of age he began to preach in private and public gatherings. His influence became very great, such was his reputation for piety and his success in talking, preaching, and writing concerning spiritual matters. He wrote 111 hymns, most of which appeared in his *Spiritual Flower Garden*, 1731. He died in 1769. **Key Verse:** For your unfailing love is higher than the heavens. Your faithfulness reaches to the clouds.
–Psalm 108:4

♦ 108 ♦

ALL GLORY, LAUD AND HONOR
> *Refrain*
> *All glory, laud and honor,*
> *To Thee, Redeemer, King,*
> *To Whom the lips of children*
> *Made sweet hosannas ring.*

Thou art the King of Israel,
Thou David's royal Son,
Who in the Lord's Name comest,
The King and Blessed One. *Refrain*

The company of angels
Are praising Thee on High,
And mortal men and all things
Created make reply. *Refrain*

To Thee, before Thy passion,
They sang their hymns of praise;
To Thee, now high exalted,
Our melody we raise. *Refrain*

Thou didst accept their praises;
Accept the prayers we bring,
Who in all good delightest,
Thou good and gracious King.
Refrain

About the writer: Theodulph is said to have been a native of Italy. The exact date of his birth is not known. He came to France in the time of Charlemagne, about 781, and was made Bishop of Orleans in 785. He was imprisoned by Louis I at Angers in 818. There are differing traditions concerning him after this period. **Key Verse:** He was in the center of the procession, and the crowds all around him were shouting, "Praise God for the Son of David! Bless the one who comes in the name of the Lord! Praise God in highest heaven!" –Matthew 21:9

♦ 109 ♦

I HEARD A SOUND OF VOICES

I heard a sound of voices,
Around the great white throne,
With harpers harping on their harps
To Him that sat thereon:
"Salvation, glory, honor!"
I heard the song arise,
As through the courts of
    heaven it rolled
In wondrous harmonies.

I saw the holy city,
The New Jerusalem,
Come down from Heav'n,
    a bride adorned
With jeweled diadem;
The flood of crystal waters
Flowed down the golden street;
And nations brought their
    honors there,
And laid them at her feet.

O great and glorious vision,
The Lamb upon His throne!
O wondrous sight for man to see!
The Savior with His own;
To drink the living waters
And stand upon the shore,
Where neither sorrow, sin nor death
Shall enter ever more.

O Lamb of God Who reignest,
Thou bright and morning Star!
Whose glory lightens that new earth
Which now we see from far;
O worthy Judge eternal,
When Thou dost bid us come,
Then open wide the gates of pearl
And call Thy servants home.

About the writer: Godfrey Thring, an English clergyman, was born in Alford, England in 1823. He graduated from Oxford in 1845 and served different charges as curate and rector until his death in 1903. He wrote many hymns and published several hymn compilations including *Hymns Congregational and Others*, 1866; *Hymns and Verses*, 1866; *Hymns and Sacred Lyrics*, 1874; and *Church of England Hymn Book*, 1880. **Key Verse:** Then I looked again, and I heard the singing of thousands and millions of angels around the throne and the living beings and the elders.
–Revelation 5:11

◆ **110** ◆

ROCK OF AGES
Rock of Ages, cleft for me,
Let me hide myself in Thee;
Let the water and the blood,
From Thy wounded side which flowed,
Be of sin the double cure;
Save from wrath and make me pure.

Not the labor of my hands
Can fulfill Thy law's demands;
Could my zeal no respite know,
Could my tears forever flow,
All for sin could not atone;
Thou must save, and Thou alone.

Nothing in my hand I bring,
Simply to the cross I cling;
Naked, come to Thee for dress;
Helpless look to Thee for grace;
Foul, I to the fountain fly;
Wash me, Savior, or I die.

While I draw this fleeting breath,
When mine eyes shall close in death,
When I soar to worlds unknown,
See Thee on Thy judgment throne,
Rock of Ages, cleft for me,
Let me hide myself in Thee.

About the writer: Augustus Montague Toplady was born in Surrey, England in 1740. His father was an officer in the British army. His mother was a woman of great piety. He prepared for the university at Westminster School and graduated from Trinity College, Dublin. While on a visit to Ireland at the age of 16 he converted to Christianity at a service held in a barn. The preacher was an illiterate but warm-hearted layman. Concerning this experience

Toplady wrote: "Strange that I, who had so long sat under the means of grace in England, should be brought nigh unto God in an obscure part of Ireland, amidst a handful of God's people met together in a barn, and under the ministry of one who could hardly spell his name. Surely this is the Lord's doing, and it is marvelous." He was ordained to the ministry in the Church of England in 1762 and in 1768 he became vicar of Broadhembury, a position he held until his death. A short time before he died he asked his physician what he thought. The reply was that his pulse showed that his heart was beating weaker every day. Toplady replied with a smile: "Why, that is a good sign that my death is fast approaching; and, blessed be God, I can add that my heart beats stronger and stronger every day for glory." He died in 1778. His volume of *Psalms and Hymns for Public and Private Worship* was published in 1776. **Key Verse:** Trust in the LORD always, for the LORD GOD is the eternal Rock. –Isaiah 26:4

◆ 111 ◆

SWEET HOUR OF PRAYER
Sweet hour of prayer! sweet hour of prayer!
That calls me from a world of care,
And bids me at my Father's throne
Make all my wants and wishes known.
In seasons of distress and grief,
My soul has often found relief
And oft escaped the tempter's snare
By thy return, sweet hour of prayer!

Sweet hour of prayer! sweet hour of prayer!
The joys I feel, the bliss I share,
Of those whose anxious spirits burn
With strong desires for thy return!
With such I hasten to the place
Where God my Savior shows His face,
And gladly take my station there,
And wait for thee, sweet hour of prayer!

Sweet hour of prayer! sweet hour of prayer!
Thy wings shall my petition bear
To Him whose truth and faithfulness
Engage the waiting soul to bless.
And since He bids me seek His face,
Believe His Word and trust His grace,
I'll cast on Him my every care,
And wait for thee, sweet hour of prayer!

Sweet hour of prayer! sweet hour of prayer!
May I thy consolation share,
Till, from Mount Pisgah's lofty height,
I view my home and take my flight:
This robe of flesh I'll drop and rise
To seize the everlasting prize;
And shout, while passing through the air,
"Farewell, farewell, sweet hour of prayer!"

About the writer: William W. Walford was a blind English preacher. "Sweet hour of prayer" first appeared in print in the *New York Observer* in 1845. The unknown contributor who furnished the hymn wrote, "During my residence at Coleshill, Warwickshire, England, I became acquainted with W.W. Walford, the blind preacher, a man of obscure birth and connections and no education, but of strong mind and most retentive memory. In the pulpit he never failed to select a lesson well adapted to his subject, giving chapter and verse with unerring precision, and scarcely ever misplacing a word in his repetition of the Psalms, every part of the New Testament, the prophecies, and some of the histories, so as to have the reputation of knowing the whole Bible by heart. I rapidly copied the lines with my pencil as he uttered them, and send them for insertion in the *Observer* if you think them worthy of preservation." **Key Verse:** Keep on praying.
–1 Thessalonians 5:17

❖ 112 ❖

IN HEAVENLY LOVE ABIDING
In heavenly love abiding, no change my heart shall fear.
And safe in such confiding, for nothing changes here.
The storm may roar without me, my heart may low be laid,
But God is round about me, and can I be dismayed?

Wherever He may guide me, no want shall turn me back.
My Shepherd is beside me, and nothing can I lack.
His wisdom ever waking, His sight is never dim.
He knows the way He's taking, and I will walk with Him

Green pastures are before me, which yet I have not seen.
Bright skies will soon be over me, where darkest clouds have been.
My hope I cannot measure, my path to life is free.
My Savior has my treasure, and He will walk with me.

About the writer: Anna Waring was born in Southern Wales in 1820. Her *Hymns and Meditations* were published in London in 1853. Very little is known about her life. **Key Verse:** Even when I walk through the dark valley of death, I will not be afraid, for you are close beside me. Your rod and your staff protect and comfort me. –Psalm 23:4

❖ 113 ❖

JESUS LOVES ME
Jesus loves me! This I know,
For the Bible tells me so.
Little ones to Him belong;
They are weak, but He is strong.
> *Refrain*
> *Yes, Jesus loves me!*
> *Yes, Jesus loves me!*
> *Yes, Jesus loves me!*
> *The Bible tells me so.*

Jesus loves me! This I know,
As He loved so long ago,
Taking children on His knee,
Saying, "Let them come to Me."
Refrain

Jesus loves me still today,
Walking with me on my way,
Wanting as a friend to give
Light and love to all who live. *Refrain*

Jesus loves me! He who died
Heaven's gate to open wide;
He will wash away my sin,
Let His little child come in. *Refrain*

Jesus loves me! He will stay
Close beside me all the way;
Thou hast bled and died for me,
I will henceforth live for Thee. *Refrain*

About the writer: Anna Bartlett Warner was born in 1820 in West Point, New York. Her novel *Say and Seal*, 1859, prepared in association with her sister Susan, contains the poem "Jesus Loves Me." In the book the words are spoken to a dying child. From this perspective, there is another, very moving stanza not commonly found in hymnals: Jesus loves me! Loves me still, / Though I'm very weak and ill, / That I might from sin be free / Bled and died upon the tree. **Key Verses:** And I pray that Christ will be more and more at home in your hearts as you trust in him. May your roots go down deep into the soil of God's marvelous love. And may you have the power to understand, as all God's people should, how wide, how long, how high, and how deep his love really is. –Ephesians 3:17, 18

♦ 114 ♦
WHEN I SURVEY THE WONDROUS CROSS
When I survey the wondrous cross
On which the Prince of glory died,
My richest gain I count but loss,
And pour contempt on all my pride.

Forbid it, Lord, that I should boast,
Save in the death of Christ my God!
All the vain things that charm me most,
I sacrifice them to His blood.

See from His head, His hands, His feet,
Sorrow and love flow mingled down!

Did e'er such love and sorrow meet,
Or thorns compose so rich a crown?

Were the whole realm of nature mine,
That were a present far too small;
Love so amazing, so divine,
Demands my soul, my life, my all.

About the writer: Isaac Watts is considered the father of English hymnody. He was born in Southampton, England in 1674. He was a precocious child who learned to read almost as soon as he could speak and wrote verses while still a young boy. He was firmly attached to the principles of the Nonconformists, for which his father had suffered imprisonment, and was therefore compelled to decline the advantages of the great English universities, which at that time received only Church of England students. He attended instead the Dissenting academy in London. In 1705 he published his first volume of poems, *Horae Lyricae*, which was widely praised. His *Hymns and Spiritual Songs* appeared in 1707; *Psalms*, in 1719; and *Divine Songs for Children*, in 1720. He became pastor of an Independent Church in London in 1702 but was so frail due to ill health that much of the time the work of the parish was done by an assistant. He died in 1748 and was buried in Westminster Abbey. **Key Verse:** As for me, God forbid that I should boast about anything except the cross of our Lord Jesus Christ. Because of that cross, my interest in this world died long ago, and the world's interest in me is also long dead. –Galatians 6:14

◆ **115** ◆

O FOR A THOUSAND TONGUES TO SING
O for a thousand tongues to sing
My great Redeemer's praise,
The glories of my God and King,
The triumphs of His grace!
My gracious Master and my God,
Assist me to proclaim,
To spread through all the earth abroad
The honors of Thy name.

Jesus! the name that charms our fears,
That bids our sorrows cease;
'Tis music in the sinner's ears,
'Tis life, and health, and peace.
He breaks the power of canceled sin,
He sets the prisoner free;
His blood can make the foulest clean,
His blood availed for me.

In Christ your Head, you then shall know,
Shall feel your sins forgiven;
Anticipate your heaven below,
And own that love is heaven.
Glory to God, and praise and love
Be ever, ever given,
By saints below and saints above,
The church in earth and heaven.

On this glad day the glorious Sun
Of Righteousness arose;
On my benighted soul He shone
And filled it with repose.
Sudden expired the legal strife,
'Twas then I ceased to grieve;
My second, real, living life
I then began to live.

Then with my heart I first believed,
Believed with faith divine,
Power with the Holy Ghost received
To call the Savior mine.
I felt my Lord's atoning blood
Close to my soul applied;
Me, me He loved, the Son of God,
For me, for me He died!

See all your sins on Jesus laid:
The Lamb of God was slain,
His soul was once an offering made
For every soul of man.
Awake from guilty nature's sleep,
And Christ shall give you light,
Cast all your sins into the deep,
And wash the soul white.

Harlots and publicans and thieves
In holy triumph join!
Saved is the sinner that believes
From crimes as great as mine.
With me, your chief, ye then shall know,
Shall feel your sins forgiven;
Anticipate your heaven below,
And own that love is heaven.

About the writer: Charles Wesley has been called "the poet of Methodism." Born in Epworth, England in 1707 he was educated at Westminster School and Oxford University, where he took his degree in 1728. It was while a student at Christ Church College that Wesley and a few associates, by strict attention to duty and exemplary conduct, won for themselves the derisive epithet of "Methodists." He was ordained a priest in the Church of England in 1735, and that same year he sailed with his brother John as a missionary to Georgia. They soon returned to England. He was not converted, according to his own convictions, until Whitsunday, May 21, 1738. On that day he received a conscious knowledge of sins forgiven, and this event was the real beginning of his mission as the singer of Methodism. His hymns can generally be classified as hymns of Christian experience ("O for a Thousand Tongues to Sing"); invitation hymns ("Come, Sinners, to the Gospel Feast"); sanctification hymns ("O for a Heart to Praise My God"); funeral hymns ("Rejoice for a Brother Deceased"); and hymns on the love of God ("Wrestling Jacob"). He was not a singer alone, but as an itinerant preacher he was a busy and earnest co-laborer with his brother. After his marriage, in 1749, his itinerant labors were largely restricted to London and Bristol. He died in

1788. Incredibly he wrote more than 6,500 hymns. **Key Verse:** Then I looked again, and I heard the singing of thousands and millions of angels around the throne and the living beings and the elders. –Revelation 5:11

♦ 116 ♦

WE LIFT OUR HEARTS TO THEE

We lift our hearts to Thee,
O Day Star from on high!
The sun itself is but Thy shade,
Yet cheers both earth and sky.

O let Thine orient beams
The night of sin disperse,
The mists of error and of vice
Which shade the universe.

May we this life improve,
To mourn for errors past;
And live this short, revolving day
As if it were our last.

To God—the Father, Son,
And Spirit—One in Three,
Be glory; as it was, is now,
And shall forever be.

About the writer: John Wesley was born at the Epworth rectory in 1703. He went to Oxford University in 1720 and was ordained deacon in 1725. He returned to Oxford in 1729 and became leader of the "holy club" or Methodists which had been organized during his absence by his brother, Charles. He went to Georgia as a missionary in 1735 and while there published his first hymn book. He returned to England at the end of two years, saying: "I went to America to convert the Indians, but O who shall convert me? Who is he that will deliver me from this evil heart of unbelief?" He had been impressed by the piety and faith of the Moravians in a storm while crossing the ocean, and they now became his spiritual guides. While attending one of their prayer meetings on May 24, 1738, he obtained the conscious knowledge of sins forgiven and of his acceptance with God. From this time until his death in 1791 he was unremitting in his labors as a preacher. **Key Verse:** Let us lift our hearts and hands to God in heaven. –Lamentations 3:41a

♦ 117 ♦

THE LORD OUR GOD IS CLOTHED WITH MIGHT

The Lord our God is clothed with might,
The winds obey His will;

He speaks, and in His heavenly height,
He speaks, and in His heavenly height,
The rolling sun stands still.

Rebel, ye waves, and o'er the land
With threatening aspect roar;
The Lord uplifts His awful hand,
The Lord uplifts His awful hand,
And chains you to the shore.

Ye winds of night, your force combine;
Without His high behest,
Ye shall not, in the mountain pine,
Ye shall not, in the mountain pine,
Disturb the sparrow's rest.

Ye nations, bend, in reverence bend;
Ye monarchs, wait His nod;
And bid the choral song ascend
And bid the choral song ascend
To celebrate our God.

About the writer: Henry Kirke White, a gifted English poet who died early
in life, was born in Nottingham, England in 1785. Very early he demonstrated
a love for books and a talent for composition. But his parents were poor and
he was apprenticed to a stocking weaver. He later left and began the study of
law. His conversion from deism to Christianity brought him to St. John's
College, Cambridge to prepare for the ministry. He died suddenly in 1806, in
the second year of his college courses, when only 21 years of age. Prior to his
death, in 1803, he published a small volume of poems that shared his victory
over skepticism and subsequent faith and piety. **Key Verse:** The mighty
God, the LORD, has spoken; he has summoned all humanity from east to
west! –Psalm 50:1

◆ **118** ◆

I BOW MY FOREHEAD TO THE DUST
I bow my forehead to the dust,
I veil mine eyes for shame,
And urge, in trembling self distrust,
A prayer without a claim.
No offering of mine own I have,
Nor works my faith to prove;
I can but give the gifts He gave,
And plead His love for love.

I dimly guess, from blessings known,
Of greater out of sight;
And, with the chastened psalmist, own
His judgments too are right.
And if my heart and flesh are weak
To bear an untried pain,
The bruiséd reed He will not break,
But strengthen and sustain.

I know not what the future hath
Of marvel or surprise,
Assured alone that life and death
His mercy underlies.
And so beside the silent sea
I wait the muffled oar;
No harm from Him can come to me
On ocean or on shore.

I know not where His islands lift
Their fronded palms in air;
I only know I cannot drift
Beyond His love and care;
And Thou, O Lord, by Whom are seen
Thy creatures as they be,

Forgive me if too close I lean
My human heart on Thee.

About the writer: John Greenleaf Whittier, commonly known as the "Quaker Poet," was born in Haverhill, Massachusetts in 1807. Beginning life as a farm boy and village shoemaker, and with only a limited education, he entered the profession of journalism in 1828. He became that year editor of the *American Manufacturer* and, in 1830, editor of the *New England Review*. In 1836 he became Secretary of the American Anti-Slavery Society and editor of its official publication, the *Freeman*. In his religious poems he always magnified the goodness and love of God for humanity and the need for Christian charity. From 1824 until his death in 1892 he wrote and published poems singly in periodicals and collectively in book form. From these poems about 75 hymns have been made by selecting verses of religious and devotional sentiments. **Key Verse:** I take back everything I said, and I sit in dust and ashes to show my repentance. –Job 42:6

◆ 119 ◆

GUIDE ME, O THOU GREAT REDEEMER
Guide me, O Thou great Redeemer
Pilgrim through this barren land.
I am weak, but Thou art mighty;
Hold me with Thy powerful hand.
Bread of heaven, bread of heaven,
Feed me till I want no more;
Feed me till I want no more.

Open now the crystal fountain,
Whence the healing stream doth flow;
Let the fire and cloudy pillar
Lead me all my journey through.
Strong Deliverer, strong Deliverer,
Be Thou still my Strength and Shield;
Be Thou still my Strength and Shield.

When I tread the verge of Jordan,
Bid my anxious fears subside;
Death of deaths, and hell's destruction,
Land me safe on Canaan's side.
Songs of praises, songs of praises,
I will ever give to Thee;
I will ever give to Thee.

Musing on my habitation,
Musing on my heav'nly home,
Fills my soul with holy longings:
Come, my Jesus, quickly come;
Vanity is all I see;
Lord, I long to be with Thee!
Lord, I long to be with Thee!

About the writer: William Williams has been called "the Watts of Wales." Born in 1717, his "awakening" was due to an open-air sermon by the famous Welsh preacher, Howell Harris. Williams received deacon's orders in the Established Church, but subsequently became a Calvinistic Methodist preacher. As an evangelistic preacher he was popular and successful among the Welsh. He died in 1791. **Key Verse:** The LORD guided them by a pillar of cloud during the day and a pillar of fire at night. That way they could travel whether it was day or night. –Exodus 13:21

◆ 120 ◆

SHALL I, FOR FEAR OF FEEBLE MAN

Shall I, for fear of feeble man,
The Spirit's course in me restrain?
Or, undismayed, in deed and word
Be a true witness for my Lord?

Awed by a mortal's frown, shall I
Conceal the Word of God most high?
How then before Thee shall I dare
To stand, or how Thine anger bear?

Savior of men, Thy searching eye
Doth all my inmost thoughts descry;
Doth aught on earth my wishes raise,
Or the world's pleasures,
    or its praise?

The love of Christ doth me constrain
To seek the wandering souls of men;
With cries, entreaties, tears, to save,
To snatch them from
      the gaping grave.

Give me Thy strength,
      O God of power;
Then let winds blow,
      or thunders roar,
Thy faithful witness will I be:
'Tis fixed; I can do all through Thee!

About the Writer: John Joseph Winckler, a German Pietist, was born in Saxony in 1670. He was at first a pastor at Magdeburg, then a chaplain in the Protestant army, accompanying the troops to Holland and Italy. He was known for his great courage and convictions. He died in 1722. **Key Verse:** A truthful witness saves lives, but a false witness is a traitor. –Proverbs 14:25

◆ 121 ◆

CHRIST FOR THE WORLD WE SING
Christ for the world we sing,
The world to Christ we bring, with loving zeal,
The poor and them that mourn, the faint and overborne,
Sin sick and sorrow worn, whom Christ doth heal.

Christ for the world we sing,
The world to Christ we bring, with fervent prayer;
The wayward and the lost, by restless passions tossed,
Redeemed at countless cost, from dark despair.

Christ for the world we sing,
The world to Christ we bring, with one accord;
With us the work to share, with us reproach to dare,
With us the cross to bear, for Christ our Lord.

Christ for the world we sing,
The world to Christ we bring, with joyful song;
The newborn souls, whose days, reclaimed from error's ways,
Inspired with hope and praise, to Christ belong.

About the writer: Samuel Wolcott, a Congregational clergyman, was born in South Windsor, Connecticut in 1813. He graduated from Yale in 1833 and Andover Theological Seminary in 1837. He was a missionary in Syria; served as a pastor in various towns and cities, including Providence and Chicago; and later became Secretary of the Ohio Home Missionary Society. He died in 1886. All 200 of his hymns were written later in life after he retired. **Key Verse:** In every nation he accepts those who fear him and do what is right. —Acts 10:35

+ **122** +

HOLY, HOLY, HOLY, LORD

Holy, holy, holy, Lord
God of Hosts, eternal King,
By the heavens and earth adored!
Angels and archangels sing,
Chanting everlastingly
To the Blessed Trinity.

Cherubim and seraphim
Veil their faces with their wings;
Eyes of angels are too dim
To behold the King of kings,
While they sing eternally
To the Blessed Trinity.

Since by Thee were all things made,
And in Thee do all things live,
Be to Thee all honor paid;
Praise to Thee let all things give;
Singing everlastingly
To the Blessed Trinity.

Hallelujah! Lord, to Thee
Father, Son and Holy Ghost,
Godhead one, and Persons three,
Join we with the heavenly host,
Singing everlastingly
To the Blessed Trinity.

About the writer: Christopher Wordsworth was born in Lambeth, England in 1807. At Trinity College, Cambridge he won numerous university honors before graduating in 1830. In 1836 he became headmaster of Harrow School and was later appointed a canon of Westminster, in 1844. He was appointed Bishop of Lincoln in 1869, which office he held for fifteen years, resigning only a few months before his death in 1885. He was a nephew of the poet William Wordsworth. He was a voluminous writer, among his works being a *Commentary on the Whole Bible* (1856-1870), a *Church History* (1881-1883), and a volume of hymns titled *The Holy Year*. He wrote over 125 hymns in his lifetime. **Key Verse:** In a great chorus they sang, "Holy, holy, holy is the LORD Almighty! The whole earth is filled with his glory!" –Isaiah 6:3

◆ 123 ◆

JESUS, THY BLOOD AND RIGHTEOUSNESS

Jesus, Thy blood and righteousness
My beauty are, my glorious dress;
'Midst flaming worlds,
    in these arrayed,
With joy shall I lift up my head.

Lord, I believe Thy precious blood,
Which, at the mercy seat of God,
Forever doth for sinners plead,
For me, e'en for my soul, was shed.

Jesus, the endless praise to Thee,
Whose boundless mercy
      hath for me—
For me a full atonement made,
An everlasting ransom paid.

O let the dead now hear Thy voice;
Now bid Thy banished ones rejoice;
Their beauty this,
    their glorious dress,
Jesus, Thy blood and righteousness.

About the writer: Count Nicolaus Ludwig Zinzendorf, the founder of the religious community of Herrnhut and the apostle of the United Brethren, was born in Dresden in1700. It is not often that noble blood and worldly wealth are allied with true piety and missionary zeal. Such, however, was the case with Count Zinzendorf. In 1731 Zinzendorf resigned all public duties and devoted himself to missionary work. He traveled extensively on the Continent, in Great Britain, and in America, preaching "Christ, and him crucified," and organizing societies of Moravian brethren. John Wesley is said to have been under obligation to Zinzendorf for some ideas on singing, organization of classes, and church government. Zinzendorf was the author of some 2,000 hymns. He died at Herrnhut in 1760. **Key Verse:** Yet now God in his gracious kindness declares us not guilty. He has done this through Christ Jesus, who has freed us by taking away our sins. –Romans 3:24